"Debra has produced a powerful modern handbook that guides us through ancient wisdom teachings. The four elements, the four directions are the cornerstones to the wisdom of the elders. All of us need to be reminded of what we have forgotten, so that we may dream a new world into being."

—*Alberto Villoldo PhD*
author of *Shaman, Healer, Sage*

"Debra Silverman stood out in the midst of an endless sea of coaches, therapists and healers. From our very first meeting I felt like she knew and understood me; she has been offering me practical direction ever since. This book continues to do the same. Debra's work is intuitive, smart, compassionate and direct and brings the heavens right down to earth in a way that is inspiring and easy to understand. I am grateful to Debra both as a personal guide and for creating such a meaningful book. Hers is a well-needed vision in our complex times."

—*Seane Corn*
Seane Corn is an internationally renowned yoga teacher
and spiritual activist. Her DVDs include "Detox Flow Yoga."

"In the din and roar that surrounds us, we need to be centered to make decisions, pause, and listen to forces much larger than us, yet there for us…if we listen. Debra helps us listen, gently shares tools, and in this book, and her work, helps people – like myself – think and act from a place where I am connected."

—*Winona LaDuke*
Winona LaDuke is an American Indian activist,
environmentalist, economist, and writer.

May you find
Balance in your world.

Warmly,

THE
MISSING
ELEMENT

INSPIRING

COMPASSION

FOR THE HUMAN

CONDITION

DEBRA SILVERMAN M.A.

FINDHORN PRESS

Findhorn Press
One Park Street
Rochester, Vermont 05767
www.findhornpress.com

Findhorn Press is a division of Inner Traditions International

ISBN 978-1-84409-689-3

Cataloging-in-Publication Data for this title is available from the British Library

Printed and bound in the United States by Versa Press, Inc.

Edited by Hazel Dawkins
Cover design by Damian Keenan
Text design and layout by Thierry Bogliolo

All Photos © Thinkstock/GettyImages except *Namaste Man* on page 10 courtesy of Russell Bramlett

Contents

Acknowledgments

First, I thank Mom and Dad, Tillie and Milt – because of them I can write about compassion. Unfortunately their deaths are what it took to for me to understand my love for them. I offer my simple voice of gratitude to them and all parents, for it is parents who have given us the gift of life.

Next I want to thank my best friend. Just as Oprah has Gail, I have you, Laurel. Laurel holds my heart like it is golden, as if I am special. After all these years...I am beginning to believe you.

This work of art was created under the effect of pure magic – I mean it. You won't believe me when I tell you that there were four angels who appeared in my life in a two-week period. They magically financed me as a writer. I could never have afforded to write this book without your help. Without my ever asking, they appeared one by one, insisting that they help me – no strings attached. It is called angel money. I am scared that I will never know how to thank you properly and give back to each of you the way you gave to me – Janie, Paul, Wayne and Lynn. You four were the midwives to this book.

I have written this book for my son and the youth who suffer for the pain of this crazy modern world. Daniel, I can only pray and hope that you find the deep, abiding faith to believe in this world. It is just like life's sense of humor to have sent you, a serious realist, to a whimsical, esoteric astrologer like me for your mother. How ironic that between us we cover the spectrum from the ground-level, practical earth concerns that you love, to the stars and the cosmic language that I adore. I hope to meet you in between our two worlds through this lifetime, continually watching our love grow.

Thank you, Dad, Milt, who was in the Jewish Mafia, and taught me by example that "friendship is holy." I followed his lead when my family of origin broke into pieces upon his death. My friends became my family.

There are those of you who have held me through my young life who I must mention: kindergarten through high school, you guys unknowingly let me lean on you when my family was nowhere to be found: Elyse, Karen, Nancy, David, Joel, Matt, Ava and Debby. Then in later years there appeared: Alandra, Judy B and Judy K, Catherine, Gudrun, Norman, Bobbi and Richie, Victor and Nadya, and Jim. Some of you have come and gone. There are those who have never left my side: Forrest, Colette, Ellen M, Ellen F, and Grace. And thank God for my Colorado family who have provided a home to me as an adult: Lynn, Carla and Doug, Habiba and Kabir, Peggy, Dorothy, Margaret, and our beloved Douglas. Finally, those who have become home –

that I still cannot explain – fate has happily had her way with us: Paul and Adriana, June, Wayne, Teddy, Trista, Junpo and Mary, Desi, Josh, Ash and Ayelet, Bill, and Ashley and Parker.

I could not be tirelessly giving as I do in this world without each one of you having faith in me. I am coming to understand that love is no longer about family or friends or who is in and who is out. It is that we are all in this dance together. We all play our roles, for however short or however long. I pray that I can dance with you, the reader of this, some day. We will do so as the Gods and Goddesses see fit – it has become obvious to me that fate determines when and how we will find our way to each other.

There are those who have helped me write this book and have collaborated on my life's work. A long, fifteen-year arduous effort of just this writing project. Starting way back with Billie, Ammi, Sara, Stasia, Lowell, Moon, Betty, Lisa, Naomi, Dennis, Kippi, Michelle, Owen, Val, Bill, Randy, Mark, Jack, Laurie, Jenn, Hazel, and Premo.

And to Charlie, Kenny, Colette, and the Goodmans for giving me your story for this book.

And my one family member who has stood by me forever, beyond all time: that would be you, Niki.

This project has taken so long that just writing this page has been like an ant carrying a huge stone up a hill. So long up, and with so much effort, yet I could not stop.

I am here to tell all of you that dreams do come true. This book was a long-standing dream that has finally found pages, form, and feet.

Lastly, I have been carrying this dream for the future generations – the children who continually appear in my world for me to be their fairy godmother: Ligia, James, Lauren, Ryan, Bodie, Ya-ya, Talulah, Marcus, Sabrina, Shane, Sarah, Ibby, and Ocean. For all those children carrying the future, I hope that I have made your load a bit lighter. Stand on my shoulders and help us all get through this unbelievable time in history.

P.S. And special thanks to Sting and Madonna. I was the same astrologer the day before I met you, but you both became a doorway that has helped my cause. My deepest appreciation to you, Stingo. You truly are my friend.

To all of you who, for almost four decades, have sought me out and invited me to sit next to you as you opened up to your depths and shared your life story. I have loved listening to you.

I adore humans – I carry an unabashed love for the victors who made it through their pain, and as well for the perpetrators who created it.
Evil has no power over the compassion I feel for humanity.
My prayer is that we as a species will survive this narrow entrance into the next age, and that many more of us will touch the sweet spot of our humility.
With the long view intact, we will come to understand our humanness as a long, unfolding experiment that is about to turn a corner.

I pray this book inspires compassion as you and your observer look at yourself and others. This is the doorway to the golden age and the future is depending on us.

Prologue

WE ARE MISSING THE WISDOM OF THE ELDERS

I've got good news and bad news, so let's get the bad news out of the way. We do not have enough oil, clean air, water and gas to support the number of people on our planet. We do not know how to distribute wealth or food to those in need. We do not know how to banish genocide, child slavery, drug cartels, sex trade, war, or evil. Those are big, big problems and they're overwhelming to think about. People ask me all the time, "What can I do to make a difference?"

That's what this book is about. You! Wonderfully flawed, perfectly nutty, beautiful, broken-hearted, powerful you. Would you like to impact the planet and be a part of a positive change? Would you like to feel more at peace with yourself and be a happier human being?

Here's the good news: global change begins at home.

Yes, recycling and saving water is very important, but your big job is to open your eyes to who you truly are – warts and all – and to make peace with that clunky, wonderful person inside of you. If you can do this, then all the negativity, fear and shame that block your authentic expression will begin to lift and you can become a more powerful, effective human being on this planet.

That's how we begin to change the world. We heal one person at a time, and we start with ourselves.

Wisdom of the Elders

A body of wisdom exists that is based on many ancient cultures. American Indians prayed to the *Four Directions*. Kabalistic Jews spoke of the *Four Worlds*. The Hawaiian Hula culture immersed itself in the *Four Elements*. Buddhists wrote the *Four Noble Truths*. And the Egyptians passed on to us their version of the *Four Elements*, which is steeped in astrology – the oldest science on earth. These people honored the land they lived on – not because it was a good idea, but because they were dependent on it for their survival and they had to pay attention. They operated with rocks in their pockets and wisdom in their hearts.

These cultures cultivated a long view of seeing the world, and used a distant "Observer" position to avoid becoming mired in the myopic vantage point we call ego. The elders of the American Indian and Chinese cultures looked seven generations ahead as they made their decisions. We have neglected such wisdom, living more from what will make us happy today, rather than what will bring peace to our great-great-grandchildren and their grandchildren.

As an astrologer, I can tell you that we are living in a time period that the prophets foresaw. The Mayans, the Eastern Indians who wrote about the Kali Yuga, the Hopis, and the Incas – all of these ancient seers knew what was coming and wanted to be here for this transition. It's no wonder that when this book was published, our population had reached a climax of seven billion. Everyone you ever knew is here.

This is a time in history like no other. Never before could we read the news with the touch of a button. In the past, a ship sailed across the ocean with a message that was no longer news. The elders carried rocks in their pockets; we carry lightweight electronic devices.

Yet we are walking toward failure – and this too was predicted. Egypt, Greece, Rome, Great Britain: the rise and fall of these cultures is well documented; each was left in dust and ruins. We in the United States are experiencing a huge shift, and if we do not respond to the changes at hand, our status as a super-power will be threatened… not that that's a bad thing – I'm just saying change is upon us and we need to pay attention.

One of the biggest problems is that as a modern species we've become accustomed to a much easier life. We are addicted to comfort and convenience. We do not like change. We do not *want* change and yet we must.

Hard Truths and the Voice of Hope

While we are a highly evolved, technological species, let me speak to the unspeakable: we are primitive and stupid. We are destroying our planet and at the same time inventing countless ways to heal her. We have great difficulty getting out of emotional depression, exercising regularly, or eating nutritiously. Yet we have mountains of research that inform us how to be healthy. We know what we ought to do. We are overwhelmed by the screaming demand for change – and we are terrified of it. Organizations everywhere are inspiring a different future and doing great work, and just as many governmental agencies are dinosaurs resisting these new ideas.

The world economy is changing. We're depleting our resources. The value of our currency is shifting. Environmental concerns are growing. Yet we want to maintain business as usual. We pretend all is well.

Another Hard Truth: It is scientifically questionable whether we will survive. The glaciers are shrinking at alarming rates. The planet is getting hotter. It doesn't matter what is making this happen, but scientifically it is a fact. We are melting, and there may not be much we can do about it. Scientists say we are about to pass the possibility for reversing the effects of the warming.

Hard question: What are we leaving for our kids? Here we are, waiting, at the edge of our seats, popcorn in hand, curious: Can we shift the old paradigm? Will the human condition reach a threshold of real change?

Time is our best teacher. Sometimes it requires hardship to learn, to change, and grow. However, when mixed with enough insight, even the hard can become soft. Crises such as earthquakes, heartbreaks, health issues, and financial problems present opportunities for us to open up, reach out, and receive help. Pain is a doorway to humility and wisdom, and there is plenty of personal pain and global pain to keep us busy. The doorway is wide open.

"There are two types of people in this world, those who are humble
and those who are about to be."

—Anonymous

In a time when so many new age principles tell us to stay positive at all costs – not to speak about the negative, I am asking you to do just the opposite.

Let's face the truth about the way each one of us lives, acknowledge where we aren't living in integrity, and then step away from any negative judgment so we can change – not through shame, but from love and compassion for ourselves and the human condition. We are who we are. We need to honor our human nature without judgment so that we can live from a more authentic place.

Your Elemental Mission

I want to enroll you as an agent of change – and you'll need two things. One is to become acquainted with the Four Elements as they exist inside you. The other is to cultivate the Observer's position so that you can stand back and make change by altering the way you see and live your own story.

The Four Elements

- **WATER:** For nine months we surrendered to the awesome feminine power of a womb filled with fluid. Herein lies the wisdom of *silence* and *trust*.

- **AIR:** Air is everywhere – the universal source of breath and language. No one can live without breathing or communicating. Herein lies the wisdom of *wonder* and *consciousness*.

- **EARTH:** The patience of a mountain, the generosity of a tree. Earth is the immovable rock, tirelessly waiting for our respect. Will we care for her? If we don't, don't worry: she will survive. We may not. Herein lies the wisdom of *respect* and *balance*.

- **FIRE:** The heat of your heart and the fire of the sun drive your destiny each day. We cannot live without either. Herein lies the wisdom of accepting your mission *with full conviction*.

Learning to Change

Modern life is stalking us to change. With so many books of this kind being read, spirituality has never been as popular and commonplace. As individuals and as a species we are growing. It's an unfortunate truth that we learn the most through mistakes.

It is easy to judge humanity, our neighbors, our human nature, and our own idiosyncrasies. We have danced with evil, played with guns, tried to control and scare the Feminine into submission, and nearly destroyed the Earth. Evolution occurs by learning through our mistakes, and we have a long history of making mistakes: nuclear bombs, the holocaust, 9/11, countless wars, to mention only a few examples. Can we forgive human nature, the species, and its long path down evolution lane? Would I love to change the way we learn our lessons? You bet I would. Would I love to assist people to learn the easy way? Sure.

As a parent I want to offer a positive future to my kids. I have written this book to share what I have found that holds wisdom and hope. What I'm calling the Missing Element is twofold: 1) it is the Observer inside you – the part of you that can stand outside of judgment and see yourself with a more wise and compassionate approach – much like our elders did. And 2) the

Missing Element also refers to the Elements that make up your personality and more specifically, the Element which is your weakest. Allow me to help you to see through the eyes of love. All is well, and we are exactly where the prophets of old predicted we would be – that we would reach a time when we had to get on our knees and return to basics. Water is wet, fire is hot, earth is heavy, and air is everywhere.

Read and participate in this book's exercises and examples to learn how to get back to ground level and rekindle the wisdom of the elements. This is the voice of hope.

The Good News: You have the personal power to make a difference. The power to create change resides inside you. It's so much simpler than you know. And it starts with you.

Introduction

What if I were to tell you that the parts of your personality that you dislike the most, the weirdest, quirkiest, most unlovable parts that you're certain, if seen by others, will leave you friendless, jobless and unloved, are the very doorways to your inner peace and happiness?

What if I were to tell you that everything you think is wrong with you is actually right, and all you need is permission to let those shameful, hidden parts out so you can finally be free to be authentically who you are? And what if I were to tell you that learning to be authentically who you are is an important part in healing our world?

It's all backwards. Most of us were brought up to act like nice, civilized boys and girls, and to hide the aspects of ourselves that might be inappropriate or might upset people. It's not a bad survival tactic if you don't mind being in pain much of the time – which is what it's like when you're only letting your so-called *good* side show.

The parts of you that are eccentric or rebellious, the parts that laugh too loud or cry too much…good luck trying to hold those parts in without side effects.

This is a book that flies in the face of all that early training on how to be "normal," which is just a setting on the dryer as far as I'm concerned. In all my years in private practice, I haven't met one normal person yet. Not one.

This is a story about giving yourself permission to lean into the hardest, most unloved parts of who you are, and give them some airtime – which from where I sit as a therapist-astrologer is the key to your freedom, your birthright.

It's all about the elements. You, me, and everyone else walking around the planet are made of four basic elements – Water, Air, Earth, and Fire. When we're in pain, it means these elements are out of balance in our lives. The key is to be able to discern and tag your unique style. You might be a Watery, emotional, feeling kind of person who doesn't always feel comfortable with her voice – her Air. Or maybe you're an Earthy type who needs to clean and organize before you ever leave the house in order to feel sane, and who misses the fun in life – your Fire.

It doesn't matter which personality type you have. The key is to become the Observer – to activate the aspect of yourself that just witnesses, who doesn't sit in self-judgment, but who notices who you are without trying to change you one bit. It's that simple.

Take me for example.

My personality type has a lot of Fire. That's means I'm a **big**, outgoing, bubbly girl with a huge personality. But, like a lot of fiery people, I'm also inherently shy, and I struggle with my bigness. I'm afraid I'll take over, run people down, and suck up all the energy in the room. It didn't help that there has been an attempt to shut me down in almost every relationship I have been in. So over the years, I perfected the art of holding myself back.

Imagine what it felt like to stuff all that fiery energy down? It was like having a lit firecracker in my mouth! As a kid I was certain that if I parted my lips I would burn the entire city of Detroit to the ground. So I stayed small, made safe decisions. And I suffered because I favored what I thought were my good girl parts and locked up the aspects of myself that might get me in trouble. Does this sound familiar to you? It's like favoring your left leg over your right. You'll walk funny, you'll limp, you won't be in balance.

So I played good for a long time – letting my big energy out now and again when I felt safe. This is what best friends are for; we show our real selves to those we know will love us. This is also a reason we go to therapists, to be seen and understood.

Funny enough, over the years as a therapist-astrologer, I'd noticed some-thing consistent about my clients: they all wanted to rid themselves of the parts of their personality that they disliked. That would be success for them. It was clear to me that the extent of their grief and pain was equal to how much they stifled the most natural parts of themselves. My job was to tease out these jewels, name them, and let them be celebrated.

We are who we are, right? You cannot change your stripes. And it's best to be you since everyone else is already taken. The truth is, for me, I couldn't get rid of my fiery bigness no matter how I tried – and for years and years I did.

I sought help. My therapist at the time had a great suggestion: go to a party. Not just any party, but the Thanksgiving party of a pretty famous guy I was visiting in Santa Fe. Besides the fact that I hate parties, my therapist wanted me to walk into that house and act like I owned the place. The thought of that made me want to throw up.

Clearly this was going to be a not-so-pleasant learning opportunity for me! But I was game, so I got to the party, picked up a bottle of wine from the table and started moving around the room filling people's drinks like it was **my** party. "Hi there, I'm Debra, having a good night?" I'd ask, as I cozied up to these strangers. A couple of people looked at me confused, and probably wondered who I was, but I kept pouring. Then I sat down with two men who were having what looked to be a very serious political discussion, and I jumped right in like I had been there all along, like I too had **important** things to say.

By the end of the night I was having a ball, and I realized that being in fear of my Fire was useless. The truth is, I am Fiery sometimes, and what I saw was that I was able to hold my own and I didn't burn the house down when I exposed that firecracker. After that, the judgment that I had about myself subsided and I was more balanced, free to let that part of me come out more.

What my therapist did was to help me love the part of myself that I was certain would get me killed. Now, I don't go to every party and take over, but I can if I want to, and having access to all the parts of myself means freedom, and means I'm not spending energy trying to change my true nature. Now, when I'm aware, when I'm the non-judgmental Observer, I can simply be a witness and let Debra be – and that's what I want for you.

This book will teach you about the elements, and help you reflect on aspects of your own personality and where you can strengthen the parts of your elemental nature that are out of balance. But even more important, this book is about waking up the Observer in you, so you can experience the beauty and fullness of who you are far away from judgment.

You deserve to fall in love with yourself, just as you are, in your most natural state. This love will also allow you to have compassion for other people, understanding why someone is so sensitive, or too talkative or shy, or in my case, too outgoing. Becoming the Observer inspires your compassion and nurtures your wisdom for all of us. When we aren't judging ourselves and others we are more loving. And when we are loving we take better care of ourselves and other people and the planet. We are all longing to be loved and understood. It starts with you.

Chapter 1

CRISIS

*S*ad *but true, we all grow out of the soil of pain....* The crises that arise in our lives are here to serve us, not to hurt us. As counterintuitive as this sounds, crisis is nothing more than your own soul trying to get your attention, to show you your path.

The soul uses pain, crisis, and trauma to wake us up. Who made that up?

Water is wet, fire is hot, the mango pit is too big, and your childhood was designed to introduce you to pain, death, abandonment, abuse, and heartbreak right at the start. Life doesn't care how hard your lessons are, or if you can handle them. Life just wants you to learn and to grow, and to keep your heart wide open. You are being stalked through this life to learn lessons and to pay attention to life's teachings whether you know it or not, whether you like it or not, whether you get it or not. What kind of karma are you carrying? Good karma, bad karma – too bad no one knows what that means.

Hard Truth: from birth onward you carry an invisible suitcase filled with story lines and dramas packed without your conscious remembrance. You take your first breath, then you're slapped on the bottom, and you are front-stage center – a member of the human race. Rushing toward awakening or snoring right through it – it's a choice. This is life. A breath, some karma, a body, and a big juicy story. Period. Full stop. You arrive and then here comes the wound.

Therapists make millions of dollars delving into your story's details. They help you to discover why you're suffering, and they listen attentively, looking for whom to blame, and how you came to believe your version of the tale. They help you to find solutions to make you feel better, then they happily suggest that you come back next week to deal with the next round.

Don't get me wrong, it's important to tell our stories and describe the wound – but with what intention?

The centerpiece of my psychological practice, and of other therapists who are worth their weight is: How can I help you to turn your well-worn stories into a gift and a lesson?

"The cure to pain is in the pain."

–RUMI

Your Story's Power

I've looked at the younger generation – I feel for them, this particular generation is suffering. College graduates are expected to go out into the world and be successful, loyal, reliable, kind, knowledgeable, respectful, on time, fit, beautiful, and rich. We expect you to get married, pay taxes, buy a house, go to church, never have a sexual thought about anyone but your partner, and raise perfect children. Good luck with that.

What we ought to say to our children is: Be prepared. You will fail, you will break down at some point and become overweight, addicted, and aged. Your children are going to do drugs and hurt you; some tragedy might befall them. Your parents may never understand you or even want to understand you, and you will doubt yourself every step of the way.

These are the insights I have gathered from watching human nature right up close and personal for more than three decades. I have studied you, and I am going to speak to the obvious.

We all started off determined to love our mother, father, and siblings. We accepted our childhood upbringing as "normal." It didn't matter what the story line was – how crazy or straight it was – we all had to eat, sleep, go to school, look for love, and hope that someone cared. We were forced, by circumstance, to accept our parents' reality – until we were able to leave their homes and begin our journeys as individuals. No matter where we went, we carried the imprint of our childhood.

One of the purposes of this book is to help you understand those early stories, and to ask yourself, "What is the nature of my unique personality? What am I supposed to be learning as a result of my life story? Do I have patterns that repeat themselves over and over? Do I tend to be broken-hearted? Am I always short on cash? Do I often feel unappreciated?" No matter how many spiritual books you read, crystals you hold, or green protein powder you drink, you cannot be freed of your story without identifying your broken record and becoming conscious of how it limits or supports you. You are who you are – it's not about changing your own nature, it is about rewriting the story, embracing your shadow with compassion, so that you can bless this life and live in gratitude, as a kind, loving being.

I can confidently tell you this: wherever your greatest pain lives – whatever story that follows you around like a boring friend that you just can't get rid of – therein lies the rocket fuel to get you to your purpose and wisdom. Your pain and your purpose are one and the same.

Personally, I consider that thinking of pain as the doorway to wisdom is a horrible idea because we're all going to resist it. No one willingly walks into hard lessons. Most of us deny, avoid, and drive as far away from pain as we can. But it doesn't matter. Pain is our primary access point for learning the important lessons. Period.

Take a moment to reflect and it's not hard to see. Every time you've experienced real pain you have entered a phase of growth. Did you learn the lesson and change your ways, or are you repeating your story over and over again?

Don't fear – your repetitive story has been perfectly designed just for you. Consider the example of the Dalai Lama. If you look at his life you will see how he was set up to learn (and then to teach us) about letting go.

He was recognized as the Dalai Lama at the age of three, and had to leave his parents' home. This is what happens with *Rinpoches* – they are taken away from their families and trained as leaders. His Holiness began his lifelong practice of "letting go" as a toddler.

As an adult, he had to let go once more when the Chinese mandated that he and his monks were no longer welcome in Tibet. They were forced to leave their temple, never to return again.

"Most of our troubles are due to our passionate desire for
and attachment to things...."
– THE DALAI LAMA

Each of us has a life built on a series of lessons. Should we learn the lessons, we become healers and teachers. If not, we remain victims and students, destined to repeat our need to learn the same lesson over and over.

One client of mine was ridiculed and beaten up in the third grade for being effeminate. He is now a third-grade teacher who watches for signs of bullying, and teaches his students the very thing that he learned first hand – that kindness and compassion are as important as math and reading. Being different was the crisis that eventually enabled him to become a joy-filled, gay man, and an excellent teacher.

What we do with our story is the key to what happens next. Since you are reading these words it means you are looking for a formula to help yourself through the pain. It takes time and maturity. The Dalai Lama left his family at the age of three. Our friend the teacher was first set up for his bullying lesson in the third grade. How old were you when the imprint of your trauma occurred?

There is no question that most of us will skid across the well-worn path of "normalcy" and bump hard into the wall of tragedy, fall apart, and then get up again. The soul is always standing by trying to get your attention.

We will all lose patience and give up. That's the "Ouch Factor," the trauma, the drama, the stupid story, the wake-up call. Some of you are in Crisis right now involving finances, heartbreak, depression, a health scare, or relationship issues. Do you have the faith to keep going? Do you trust that there is a teaching inside your tale, that it is happening for a reason and that you are right on schedule?

> *"Man needs difficulties; they are necessary for health."*
> — CARL JUNG, *THE TRANSCENDENT FUNCTION*

Crisis

Think of a time in your life when Crisis came to visit. What was the story that hit you on the side of your head? Maybe you found out that your husband was having an affair. Maybe you were diagnosed with a disease. The ego says, "My God, this is terrible! I've been rejected, I'm unlovable! God has deserted me."

"Really?' says the Observer, "Maybe this is an opportunity to challenge your faith. Maybe this is a good thing and it's time to step back, reconsider your life, seek counsel."

It's important that the story – the Crisis – be told, but not so we can cement it into reality and wear it like a badge. What if we had the wisdom to examine what happened to us from a non-judgmental place, and see how the pain presented us with an opportunity to learn and to grow? Our stories carry the perfect nutrients for the harvesting of wisdom – I promise you this is true. Our job as alchemists is to transmute pain into wisdom.

Those of us who are interested in growth and evolution are here to eat poison – the way the peacock consumes fungus from trees and then turns the poison into colors. We have a choice; to transform our pain into beauty. Some of us will choose to sleep, others will wake up inside the dream. It's a choice. You can have the life of complaining and victimization, or a life that fulfills your soul.

"We must each lead a way of life
with self-awareness and compassion,
to do as much as we can.
Then, whatever happens we will have no regrets."
—THE DALAI LAMA

Heartbreak, illness, financial despair, death, abandonment – you name it. Your job in this life is to polish and refine your stories – to grind up the hard-to-swallow, chunky bits and turn them into digestible nutrients, not just for your own evolution, but also for that of our entire species. That is why we are here. We need to grow into our humanness without judgment so we can live and contribute and love more fully.

Learning Our Lessons

Nothing is what it appears. The lessons you are carrying seem overwhelming, yet they are just what you were assigned by your soul. I know that sounds spiritual and lofty, but I promise, it's true. Once you tell your tale, you will realize, "What a story I keep telling myself! So defeating and convincing – is it true?"

When Will We Awaken?

A client of mine named Linda found out her husband was cheating on her and she was crushed by it. They had a strong picture-perfect relationship of twenty-four years, with a long record of commitment and partnership. And then he wandered outside the marriage.

Not long into the affair, she found out and confronted him. After doing the dance of denial he admitted to the affair. But he also broke down, saying the only reason he had strayed was that he felt distant from her and wanted a deeper connection. He felt a failure and experienced great remorse and pain. It was almost as if he didn't even recognize himself; he couldn't believe what he had done. I was able to facilitate a deep conversation that allowed them to heal. They used the crisis to fall back in love and were even more in touch with each other than before.

In a perfect world there would be a council of wisdom keepers at the entrance of the pain door, and you would immediately be assigned to a host of elders who specialized in enabling wisdom to be harvested from pain. When life screams your name by using Crisis to get your attention, your job is to bow your head, listen to the voice of your soul, and say: "Allow me to learn. I am on my knees." And ask for help. This might be the hardest of all: to be humble enough to seek counsel. What if this was taught to our children?

Human nature – dare I say – is stupid. We resist our soul's impulses. If Linda and her husband had been focused on what was happening between them, they would have noticed life tapping them on the shoulder. But they weren't paying attention, so the tap turned into the slap of infidelity.

What does it take for *you* to pay attention? Do you not listen to what's happening in your relationships until your partner has left you? Until the fight has broken out? Do you ignore your health until you're at the doctor's office, so exhausted and sick that you can hardly go on? The universe will increase the stakes to induce you to wake up, but it will always tap you on the shoulder first.

What I find is that crisis is almost always hidden in a relationship. At some critical point you and your partner will bump into an opportunity for a choice; to stay in or move on. Relationships are where the greatest lessons are learned, or not.

Here's another example: Marion comes to see me because she had been flirting with the idea of leaving her husband for years, and now she says she finally wants to do it. I quickly realize that Marion loves her husband, and that he loves her. She is never going to leave him. They have one of those soul connections that come with superglue. But Marion is the personality type (Earth) who complains. Nothing is ever good enough; it's a personality trait. The truth is, she cares about him, their family, and their need for security above all else.

After developing a rapport with her, I say, "Come on, sweetie. You're not going to leave your husband. Your job is to change your mind and to see your husband from a new angle. He is your ally, your teacher, your lesson." Boy, did that session change her life! I watched her change her attitude and her language and accept her fate.

The opposite is also true, when a couple comes to see me and they are so clearly incompatible with each other it might be time for them to split up. The person they originally fell in love has left the building – and they are no longer the same person that they began their movie with. I assist them in standing in the fire of hard reality and I say, "It's okay to change and it's okay to let go." Can you admit to the truth of change thereby preventing a full-blown crisis – an affair, financial ruin, closing down the friendship? You can if you can face what is, thus avoiding the crisis and completing the relationship without blame.

This is the high road of awakened beings, very rare indeed. Raise your hand if you know how to be honest and clean at the end of the cycle, or the end of a relationship or a job. I bet very few people are raising their hands.

There is always someone to blame, of course, but the truth is, the relationship is over regardless of the blame. Human nature does not know how to let go without a crisis.

If we had a circle of elders with whom we could consult, like in the days of old, we could circumvent this childlike behavior that is so dated and sad, and introduce wisdom and compassion. Acknowledge the love that was, the lessons learned, and the honest sadness that the relationship is over.

Power lies in acceptance, and in surrendering to what *is*. Human nature is immature. You can't move a mountain or change your bloodline. We cannot instantly change our patterns. What you can do is relinquish the mind's need to judge the human condition. I really do love humanity even with all our flaws, but only with a well-developed Observer can you join me. That is our topic in Chapter 2.

You need to follow your own rhythm. Some of us are fast at letting go (Air and Fire) while others drag our feet (Earth and Water) – and this is not good or bad. It's just us being ourselves.

We need to trust time and simple wisdom, to be ourselves at all costs and most importantly to know that Crisis will continue to find us in order to keep us awake. It's not easy to accept crisis as a gift. Linda and her husband did. Marion escaped a full-blown crisis by seeking counsel and collecting wisdom. What is stalking you right now? What lesson is trying to find your attention? How willing are you to ask for help?

> Years ago I made up a prayer: Let me wake up to my lessons before the alarm goes off. I want to be a soft sleeper, listening to the signs and messages presented to me before the frying pan comes to hit me on my head.

> Repeat after me: *Life has my back. It is trying to teach me the very lessons I am here to learn, even if I don't like them. Depression, weariness, disappointment, frustration, or physical pain – these will come. Life has my back.*

Personally, I am an endless optimist. When my clients come into my office with looks of confusion, I view them with delight. Even with illness and death, I know in time a gift may appear.

The human path always includes pain and darkness. Look how we are born, through pain. That's how it goes down here.

Being human means being humbled – at worst it includes humiliation. Each of us will walk down the street called Embarrassment Avenue. We may feel lost and without a rudder. But in those times when we are in it, at the deepest levels, and we are closest to our knees, our soft belly appears, open and tender. And we finally learn: *Being vulnerable takes far more courage than pretending we are strong and above it all.*

Will you willingly allow yourself to be human without shields and pretense? It's ok to admit: I am scared. I love you. I am sad. I am done.

It won't matter to the Earth whether humans wake up with a soft touch or not. Evolution will march on without us, as it did with the dinosaurs, indifferent to our pain. I like to think we're an experiment of the gods. They are watching us and wondering what path we will take. They are watching you, wondering if you are looking up and listening to your guides, spirits, angels, and wisdom.

The question is: Are you feeling the nudges and listening to the wake-up calls? Or do you need drama to get your attention?

Throughout history humans have been built for misery, depression and struggle. It is my mission to be joyful as I surrender to my authentic humanness. My favorite joke is that I am the president of the *Jews For Joy Club*. I have a hard time having sustained members. I long to find those who have chosen discipline and health – those who know how to balance pleasure and indulgence, who can embody an honest version of human and divine, and who will use their pain as a doorway to wisdom.

But first it's helpful to know what your nature is and how your stories present themselves to you.

Crisis and the Power of the Elements

If you are learning Water, you keep bumping into depression, mood swings, addiction, or just plain sadness from your childhood and its imprint.

If you are learning Air, it's hard to make decisions, stay in relationships, or decide what to be when you "grow up." These questions follow you around like the wind does the sky – and you just keep thinking about them.

If you are learning Earth, you'll get stuck in your job and in money and security issues. Your dieting and discipline come and go. And your integrity around right and wrong will be inconsistent.

And if you are learning about Fire, drama will follow you around. You are getting attacked, someone is angry at you, you are screaming at someone, and you can't sit still even when it's time to relax.

These next chapters on the Observer and the Elements will provide a chance to become conscious of your own elemental nature and your personality type. This will assist you in becoming aware of the lessons that tend to come your way.

Water Crisis

Weight problems, depression, loneliness, and drug, sex, and alcohol addictions. Living with a chronic illness or a feeling of despair. Riding emotional waves of happiness, then sadness. Feeling the collective pain, but not knowing what's happening, or misinterpreting the pain in some abstract way. When asked what's wrong, the answer is, "I don't know." A sense of emptiness and a lack of faith. Feeling pain for animals and their mistreatment. Pessimism and despair as a landing pad.

Air Crisis

Cut off feelings from people. Having friends and then losing them. Not finishing projects. Being indecisive. Changing your mind and partners without knowing why. Short-term relationships. Multiple marriages. Changeable and fickle. Not able to commit. Never knowing what you want to do with your life. Disconnection from children or parents. Caught in lies.

Earth Crisis

Not having enough pleasure or sexual fulfillment. Workaholic, yet dissatisfied with work. Never good enough. Overly responsible and never reciprocated. Complaints about having to give too much. Exhausted and sad that fulfillment is always burdened by the need for security. Bankruptcy or other financial burdens or crises caused by taking care of family members and others at your own expense.

Fire Crisis

Broken relationships that go out with a drama. Drama king/queen who exhausts others. Feeling unappreciated and attacked. Needing attention. Sexual promiscuity and addictions. Alcohol and/or fear of drugs. Crisis with the law. Feeling rejected in life and limited in success. Living beyond your means.

Chapter 2

THE OBSERVER

"The future, higher evolution will belong to those who live in joy, who share joy, and who spread joy."
—TORKOM SARAYDARIAN

Reading this book will help you to identify the two voices that make you human: your ego and its chatty, self-serving endless quirkiness, and what I'm calling the wise Observer that is patient, non-judgmental and loving. While they appear to be completely different, they actually both want the best for you, they just come at it in very different ways. The ego takes center stage; a real show stealer. It knows what you want, what you don't want, it steers you toward things that will make you happy, steers you away from things that might be upsetting. Sometimes your ego is flashy and loud, sometimes it's shy and self-conscious. It also comes with a handy chorus of inner voices that give you constant feedback, telling you how you look, what would make you look better, who loves you, who doesn't, and what you had better do in order not to get hurt. Sounds like a good friend except your ego talks shit about you as well, and has an opinion on everything you do, commenting on your latest mess-up and your latest success.

The Observer, on the other hand, patiently hangs out in the wings, waiting for an invitation to enter, whispering softly only when it has something meaningful to say.

The ego sounds awful in comparison, doesn't it? Loud, demanding, and critical. It's like the noisy barker at a carnival who never goes home because the show is never over. Not to mention that it takes everything personally; poor me, happy me, sad, overweight, skinny, ugly, good-looking, rich me – you name it. The operative word here is ME! It's got the voice of an opera singer warming up: "Me, me, me me me…." Not surprising, it's the source of all our drama. But why? Because ego wants you to feel good all the time. No judgment here – just a truth. The ego lives for sensation, attention, and good stories. The bigger your life, the better it feels. Think of it like a needy puppy. Cuddle me, love me, feed me, aren't I cute?

All this crazy drama comes from the ego's desire to protect you and keep you safe – kind of like one of those helicopter moms who tries to control their child's every move so that things go well for them. The ego is well meaning, just a little disoriented, not to mention totally fearful.

Now let's look at the Observer.

The Observer – the witness, our soul, our higher self – helps us to see things objectively, as they really are. It's a stance of both wisdom and compassion. It allows us to step off the worrisome ego stage of our lives and look back and review things from afar. From this more distant viewpoint, our dramas and stories are less compelling and distracting, and even endearing and sweet. "Aww, look what that silly ego is doing again," says the Observer. "How sweet!"

The Observer is one of the "Missing Elements" – the part of yourself that enables you to understand your quirky personality beyond judgment, as though you were an angel looking back at your human nature. Your Observer, the witness, the wise, quiet, soulful voice has the ability to teach, tame, and support your ruthless ego. When invited in, it says, "Hey, you're doing that thing again. You're lost in the drama. It's okay. Slow down. Take a breath. You're doing the best you can."

Can you feel the compassion here? No judgment, just gentle noticing.

The Observer cultivates humility and a soft approach to life. It helps you become good at saying things that your ego will cringe at such as, "I am sorry, I need help, I made a mistake and I was wrong." The Observer allows us to come out from behind the mask of the protective ego and become transparent and real. All healers or good teachers spend lots of time in the land of the Observer.

Imagine a huge, horseshoe-shaped, glass-bottomed observation deck anchored in a limestone cliff of the Grand Canyon – 4,000 feet above the chasm below. Look up, the turquoise sky appears endless and you can literally see for miles in all directions. Look down and the Colorado River appears as a slim, pea-green ribbon, and the burro-riding tourists below look smaller than fleas. It's a wonderful view, because with so much perspective you can't focus on the little things. All you see is the majesty of the view, held under a magnificent sky. This is the Observation deck where the Observer lives.

Once on deck, be prepared for the emergence of kindness, because this is what happens when you step back from trying to micromanage your every move so you'll look good. The Observer is compelled to heal, to care, to love you – unfortunately it's constantly sabotaged by the ego.

My job as a therapist and an astrologer is to assist you in falling in love with exactly who you are – your quirky, egoic personality – and also to introduce you to the partner of your dreams – your compassionate Observer who will laugh and shrug and sweetly say, "Hey, you're doing fine – try again." The fact is, you can't change who you are. Your emotional reactions and sensitivities are not going to be plucked out like an ingrown hair. We are a manufacturing agency of human nature stories. So just notice and adjust your behavior from a place of love.

You can read all the spiritual books you like, you can sit on cushions, eat brown bread, and drink protein powder, but when your ego is triggered or violated it will, without a doubt, react, throw a fit, cry, scream, hide, or ramble on depending on your personality type. Every ego on this planet has some pretty immature qualities, nothing that the Observer can't poke fun at, learn from and possibly even adjust over time.

One teacher with whom I studied said that once you develop your Observer nothing can hurt you – the ego will be quieted and calmed. Even if arrows of trauma and pain were shot in your direction and hit you, once aware, the pain would just land at your feet. She said, "No one can ever make you angry when you are in your Observer." That's not true for me.

My teacher was very spiritual, and in fact, in almost every spiritual circle and psychological model, the ego gets a bad rap. We're told to step over it, listen with our souls and to identify with our higher selves. Trying to be "good" is a great hobby – however I have a new job for you: accept the fact that you, just like everyone else, are a flawed humbled human. We all feel and we all fail. Don't fool yourself – no one is made of Teflon. I can assure you, having worked as a therapist with so many people, much of your faulty childhood sticks to you whether you know it or not. It's what shaped you and made you *you*.

We all grow up wounded in some way; we weren't seen, we felt ashamed because of the way we looked, the things we said. We were punished for upsetting our parents when all we wanted was to be loved. We live in reaction to some version of an old story year after year. We think it's real, that we really are unlovable and somehow different, so the punishment continues inside our minds.

When the relationship ends, when you are cheated on, when you lose your job or find out the sky is falling, you will react. Human nature is a reactive machine, impulsive and emotional. And funnily enough, I love this about being human. I have been shocked and amazed by human nature – when those I thought to be my best friends have suddenly become my worst enemies. I have cried an ocean from my confusion over how I could have loved so deeply and then have been forced by life to let go.

Our experience here on Earth demands that we learn to let go of our lovers, partners, best friends, parents, children, and our pets. It is painful and sad.

The Guru was found crying for days over the death of his son. His followers found him and pleaded, "Stop crying, teacher. There is no need to be sad. Let go." And he said, "Leave. I will cry for as long as I need to. It is my gift as a human." Such simple wisdom. The shortest verse in the Bible: "Jesus wept." No amount of spirituality can take away the stinger of sadness, or despair – it is a beautiful truth: we all are human and vulnerable. This is what makes us loveable.

While the ego can make things worse, turning our experiences into high drama, the Observer plays fair, and is your ticket to the land of non-judgment where you take nothing personally, especially yourself. The art is to fall in love with who you are, ego and all, and to meet ourselves and others with an open heart.

Pain serves to activate the soul. It assisted me in growing my Observer and I softened my pain by increasing my awareness that we are all in this together; each of us carries a wound that can be lifted and soothed. Everyone has the choice to harvest pain into wisdom; this is the Observer's role.

I'm asking you to practice becoming the Observer. To do this in a non-stressful time is easy and is a great practice that I strongly encourage. To do this when you are upset is not so easy. So how do we begin?

Imagine you are being trained for a government position where your job is to collect information, feel and sense what is happening, then report back to the central office with an objective review. In order to be good at your job you must remember there is a difference between a perception (the Observer's voice) and a judgment (the ego's voice). For example: You look at a burnt piece of toast. "Oh, look, the toast is burnt," says the Observer. That is a simple perception – hard, fast and factual. "You idiot, you burnt the toast again," says the ego. There is a judgment. To simply observe, to perceive what is in front of us requires neutrality. Simplicity. Just name it.

So the healing begins when we turn the Observer on, when we simply see things without judgment. "Oh, I didn't get the job." "I've gained five pounds." That's just what's so. We're human, these things happen. They only start to mean something when the ego gets involved with its scary commentary: "What were you thinking having that piece of pie?" "You are aging, you are fat!" "You suck!" – these are judgments.

What would our lives look like if we became more accepting and forgiving of our human nature? The nature of the human psyche is poorly designed.

We are flawed. We will continue to learn from our mistakes – we age, we gain weight, we hurt ourselves and others; we are human, raw, and beautiful. That's what it is to be real.

Once we begin to wake up to the compassionate Observer in ourselves, the part of us who worships the privilege to be in a body, alive and in service to humanity, then we can move beyond our personal drama and tend to selfless acts of service in a world that needs help so badly. Our purpose on Earth is to accept our humanness with an open, tender heart and evolve the species by remembering that you are a healing agent evolving for all of us. As you do your independent work of truly being yourself, we all benefit. This is the only way to a healthy future, starting *now*. It is you being *you*.

Chapter 3

It's Elemental

I want to introduce to you an extremely useful and effective model for understanding ourselves and cultivating compassion for our human nature. Though it may seem simple, it's one of the most important concepts I know. I encourage you to lean forward in your chair and read slowly. It's like learning how to read all over again. Even if you're advanced in your understanding, the basics are always worth reviewing.

Think for a moment about our four most essential needs for living. Where would we be without water to drink, air to breathe, food to eat, and the sun for warmth? These four Elements – Water, Air, Earth, and Fire – are not just fundamental, they are essential to all of life. We cannot survive – we wouldn't exist – without them. They are the holy source of our creation – the interdependent giants that glue our world together. And their powers begin from the moment of conception.

An orgasm – we all come into this life through a sexual act, with some kind of bang and release. Seminal fluid stimulates the beating heart, and life begins when it joins with the egg. Then Earth takes over. The body assumes a physical form based on hard-wiring and determined by your unique DNA, which creates your brain, your face, your organs. We live in a body of *water* for nine months, until we finally take our first breath (*air*) and enter the physical realm into the arms of a mother and a family (*earth*), where our arrival (one hopes) is celebrated (*fire*).

All four Elements are there at the start. And in the Bible – in the very first chapter – we see the same Elements, in the same order:

> In the beginning, God created the heaven and the earth. And the earth was without form, and void; and darkness was upon the face of the deep. And the Spirit of God moved upon the face of the *water*, and God said, Let there be light, and there was light (*air*). And God said, "Let the earth bring forth grass, the earth yielding seed" (*earth*). And God said, "Let there be lights in the firmament of the heaven to divide day from night; and let them be for signs, and for seasons, and for days, and years" (*fire*).

The Elements in Practice

These are some of the most important concepts I use in my psychotherapy practice – and they explain why my clients experience successes that far exceed the bounds of ordinary therapy. The Elements serve us in countless ways, from the beginning (with conception and creation) and all the way to our own funny personalities and quirky styles. We are a collection of Elemental factors that find their shape within our personalities and preferences. When the Elements are out of balance, our lives can be miserable.

Some of us cry easily – we are Watery and prone to addiction or depression and weight issues – while others love to talk and think, Air. Some of us might even think and talk so much that we become too overwhelmed to make decisions or to stay in relationships. Others use Earth – money and the outer world – to feel safe and secure, or to feel frustrated that we don't have enough, or that we're never getting it right. And then there are the athletic, loud, and Fiery characters who push, shout, and inspire us to get into our bodies and get a life – they are bossy and full of Fire. If they get out of balance, they become obsessive athletes who need to stand out and demand to be noticed.

These qualities are as old as the hills – they have lasted and will last well beyond the dinosaurs, humans, or any other species that have come and gone. The Elements are as cosmic as they are earthy, simple as they are complex. They describe our unique energies and personality types and they teach us our life lessons. They clothe our souls and dress up our personalities. Learning about them helps us to understand where to focus our energies, how to find balance, and how to better appreciate how they affect our children, spouses, partners, and best friends.

How can we see another's nature and bless it, love it, and celebrate it without annoyance or wishing for change? The real question is whether we can accept our own funny personality type that follows us everywhere, because to do so is wisdom. **Imagine if you never had to doubt yourself – if you understood your idiosyncrasies and found them endearing and even lovable?** Imagine if you looked at your sloppy child, or your perfectionist mother, and said, "Oh, that's just their Earth imbalance." Or when someone talks too much, you think, "There goes their Air." And when she doesn't talk at all, you understand it's merely her Water side coming to the forefront. She just loves to listen.

Permission slips are my specialty. I love to watch people acknowledge the reasons for their own funny personalities – and more importantly when they understand that real acceptance of their nature is the doorway to compassion.

It's not an excuse to say, "You talk a lot because you have Air," but rather it's a heightened state of the Observer to know who you are and what you're made of. The point of this book is twofold: 1) to wake up the Missing Element – the Observer in you so that you can live with more compassion for all the aspects of your personality, and 2) to help you see where you might be out of balance with your own Elemental nature – where you might have more Fire and a lot less Air, for example. So when I speak of the Missing Element, I'll often be referring to the Observer, but I'll also be referring to the Element you are weakest in and may need to strengthen.

Think of your parents – and before you go any further, realize that they did the best they could. My mother (Bette Midler's look-alike) had a lot of Fire, so she had a constant need for being noticed and standing out. That was her outward personality – dressing up in bright colors, jewelry, and make-up. That was her Fire. She also had lots of Water (we are a combination of all the Elements – we cannot live without any one of them). So she was as fiery as she was emotional. Once I understood my mother's elemental constitution, I was also able to understand that she was just being herself. It didn't provide me with the attentive Mom I needed, nor did it nourish me with the positive emotional support I craved. When I understood her dilemma, I was at least able to let go of the unproductive story I had developed over time about the two of us. I found compassion for my mom.

And this is the gift of the Elements: to understand those closest to you and to not demand that they behave differently. I had a student, John, whose father didn't speak much. When John realized his dad was lacking Air, John stopped trying to change him or demand that he talk. Instead, he learned to exist in silence with his father and realized that this, too, was a means of communicating.

This is the language of compassion that enables us to accept others instead of insisting they make impossible changes to accommodate our own nature. I hope to help you develop your Missing Element, or to quiet the overly active one, but truthfully you cannot change your stripes – your nature – without altering your authentic self or feeling awkward and untrue. We all can identify people who seem to have left their true natures behind and seem "fake" or "phony" – or just uncomfortable in their own skin – as opposed to those who seem naturally comfortable being and embodying their true selves.

Daily Cycle of the Elements

I want to provide you with practical tools to train your mind to have an objective view of yourself. I would love to have you fall in love with who you are and what you've been given as your personality.

The following are the primary properties embodying each element:

WATER – feelings

AIR – intellect

EARTH – practicality

FIRE – energy

If you have too much or too little of a particular element – which you can readily discern by reading the chapter on that element and noticing its relationship to you – your life will likely be out of balance. You'll want to grow and cultivate that underdeveloped element (or be careful not to become too preoccupied with the one that's overdeveloped) to put you back on an even keel. Like a car on the road, all four wheels must be balanced for smooth driving. Imagine each wheel as an element. If one of the tires is low, or overinflated, your vehicle will rattle and shake.

Whether or not we are aware of it, we follow elemental rhythms in our lives on a daily basis. We begin every morning with a Water cycle. We go to the "water closet" (or bathroom), where we use or eliminate water, wash our faces, take a shower. Next we make ourselves a cup of tea or coffee or have a glass of juice.

Then we check our calendars, make lists, check our e-mail – and begin the Air cycle. What is on my list today? Who do I need to call? What fell through the cracks yesterday? With whom do I need to communicate?

When we finish our list, the Earth cycle begins as we start to accomplish the items we've checked – dotting the i's, crossing the t's, and making sure everything is completed. Are we making money or losing money? Are we on schedule? We do our work and we head home. Plan your work, work your plan.

In the evening, we gather in the kitchen around the stove with a glass of wine – Fire water – to share our day. The Fire cycle continues as we sit together at the hearth, with the fire burning, and this manifests either as joy, enthusiasm, sharing, and celebration, or as frustration, anger, fighting, or complaining.

Each day we revolve around these cycles without even noticing them. They touch our lives constantly. But with language that acknowledges these cycles, we are able to move through our rhythms with more ease and consciousness.

Getting to Know the Elements

WATER is the element of meditation, stillness, and the purity of love. It is our feeling body. Water carries memories, history, and bloodlines. It is the emotional body that can carry hurt and disappointments long after the story is told. We are the echoes of our past through our ancestors' imprint.

The proper use of Water is to know how to release and forgive the past. Water, when used properly, provides spiritual depth and nurtures faith even when it is difficult to sustain hope. Emotional stability and wisdom is medicine for depression and addiction. Healthy Water allows us to be healers so that we are able to feel and process our feelings in real time without dragging the past around. Water at its best is the example set by the Dalai Lama, who forgives even those who have violated him.

HAVE YOU EVER SAT IN A ROOM full of people, feeling sensitive to the surroundings and intuitively picking up on the thoughts of others? And after socializing for a while you left the room feeling drained – and couldn't wait to get home to silence, and to recoup emotionally?

If you are WATER… you are allowed to cry, to go numb, to stand away, or to come in close and personal on your own terms – unpredictable and secretive. You can take time away from the noise and bustle, but promise to return with your loving smile and your desire to be with us just the way we are. You like quiet, and being alone, and you may be prone to depression, or overeating, or drinking. As you age, you'll become healthier and more concerned with self-care. Over time, self-acceptance will help you to realize that no one is normal – that it's acceptable to feel foreign among others. Meditation is your surest way to find peace and calm. Your biggest challenge is to learn how to ask for help.

AIR represents the mind, and our ability to speak and give language to our thoughts. It's about the stories we tell ourselves that either allow us to believe and have faith in beauty and love, or that limit our beliefs, convincing us that we are *less than*, and that we're all involved in nothing but broken relationships that are tired and dated or just plain impossible. We have the ability with our thoughts to create a world filled with peace and love – or to create a world that destroys any sense of hope. This is the old philosophical truth: *we are what we think.* Since the beginning of written language, we have valued mind over heart. Words have been used to separate us. But new understandings (developed by the Heart/Math Institute) suggest that the heart is hard-wired to the brain, and that the brain is the seat of intellect while the heart is the seat of wisdom.

HAVE YOU EVER BEEN IN A ROOM full of people where your social instincts had you going from one person to another, like a butterfly? Oh, how you love talking to new people… though you realize you've forgotten all of their names… and where did you put your keys?

With the proper use of Air, the mind speaks from the heart in a way that is authentic and honest. The correct use of Air creates an innocent, curious mind open to possibilities and subservient to divine direction, including faith in miracles.

If you are AIR… you have to talk, write, or read. You must follow your own rhythm – you are easily bored – and while you need to have people around you, they remain interesting only in short spurts, so you're unable to be part of a group for long. Freedom is your call; curiosity is your gift. Allow your fascination to direct and change you. You love to hear stories but keep things to yourself. Too much talk about yourself and you will be exposed. Too much talk and you will avoid doing. Don't just talk; follow through. You're good at details, even if you say you don't like them. You are prone to co-dependence – a gift and a curse – if you shy away from relationships, you can suffer a silent loneliness.

EARTH wants to provide and serve. Its function is to contribute and work. The Earth will survive regardless of what humans might do to it. The proper use of Earth involves a sense of philanthropy that considers generations to come. Earth's natural virtues are caring and sharing. Though this may sound like a spiritual theory, it is

HAVE YOU EVER SAT IN A ROOM full of people while looking at your watch because you have work to do? You decide to help in the kitchen, or do something useful – and out of nowhere you make a productive business contact that will support your professional path.

not. Work and service are the reasons we are on this Earth. This element can manifest as entitled, or arrogant, but it also can be the ultimate provider for the good of all – creating Heaven right here on Earth.

If you are EARTH... you are here to fix, heal, and make money to support others. You are strongly opinionated, if not quietly arrogant, and determined to do what is right. You are reliable, dependable, and possess and expect good things – though you always think you ought to do more. Those close to you flourish and feel safe. You are not open socially, except for professional reasons. You nourish your ego with the outer reflections of your accomplishments – though you're not seeking money or fame as much as a feeling of accomplishment and satisfaction from knowing that you have contributed, and that you're valuable and useful. You are kind-hearted and loyal, but if betrayed you have difficulty forgiving and forgetting.

F IRE is honest, righteous, and passionate about blunt, strong truths. We are at a critical moment in our history – a time we could judge as hopeless and irreparable. But the ruthless optimism of Fire can take us to truth and lead us to believe that nothing is wrong.

Fire is the element of indulgence for good or bad. Do you love your assignment to celebrate this life and do so with joy and enthusiasm, or do you escape and hide out? As a collective, we are in a Fire cycle – it's make-it-or-break-it. Fire doesn't care which way we go – toward creation or destruction. Fire remains constant but it does not burn itself. Fire has the courage and tenacity to stand in the face of hard truths instead of going into denial and despair – to hold onto faith so that we can come out of the ashes into a new and better world.

Fire means knowing how to use anger as a proactive impulse to create change rather than to destroy. Fire demands that we stand up in our lives with honesty and passion.

> HAVE YOU EVER SAT IN A ROOM full of people and you couldn't figure out what happened to the party? You popped open the wine, turned up the music, and shouted, "Anyone up for a party?" And when there was only one response, you left with the one other party animal and headed for the nearest pub.

If you are FIRE... you are here to inspire and tickle us. You want to make sure life is abundant, fun, and full of energy. You are always up for a party. You want to teach, or to win. You can be both loud and entertaining – or shy and reserved. You burn the candle at both ends, but you gain energy by spending energy. When you are pouring yourself into the betterment of yourself and others, you cannot go slow or do it softly. You don't care if others are angered by or jealous of you – though you might be surprised by it. You can feel justifiable anger – though you need to understand sarcasm so others won't hurt you with it.

Working on our Elemental Nature

At the end of this chapter is a brief survey related to the Elements. The survey will help establish – for you, at the present time – your relationship to each of the four Elements. Answer each question with a Yes or a No: if the statement is true at least 50% of the time, say Yes and score 1; if less than 50%, say No and score zero; and if you're undecided, score it $1/2$. A score of 7–10 means you're well immersed in that Element; if you score 6 or less, you're likely lacking in that Element.

To work toward balancing your elemental influences it's best if all the scores are about the same. Explore your internal habitual patterns, create a new practice intended to update those behaviors, and begin to develop and maintain the right balance and transform your life:

WATER **Explore:** Go inside and identify the Element's energies and patterns in your life.

AIR **Articulate:** Put words to your Elemental patterns – speak to and laugh about them with a trusted witness.

EARTH **Investigate:** Acknowledge the strengths and shadow-sides. Identify and get familiar with your Elemental lessons.

FIRE **Transform:** Begin a practice to create a new paradigm.

Remember, the goal is to keep all Four Elements in balance. As you learn to turn on your Observer, gain compassion for the human condition, and develop a new practice, you may want to retake the survey as part of your journey of transformation.

You will also find information about ways to dive deeper into each Element in the Appendix at the end of the book.

Four Elements Self-Survey

The following is a survey to establish which elements are naturally strong in your personality and which are less familiar.

Take the test and then, when reading each chapter, go back to the score and pay attention to whether it is an area you need to develop or one that is comfortable and easy to access.

The point of this book is to help you have all four elements in equal proportion and fully expressed. Having said that, no one has all four elements developed; there is always a missing element, and one or two that are effortless and strong. Just like the analogy of four wheels on a car needing to be balanced for an easy ride, so it is true also that all four elements in you work best when they are equally balanced.

The test results will change over time. There are times in life when one of the elements is needed. For example, shortly after having a baby, a new mother will spend months seeking quiet and peace for the baby. Water becomes the primary element. Or Earth becomes strong when you just start a new job, and details and precision are required. So our elemental constitution changes. As you learn how to balance all four parts of your personality you will notice how much easier manifestation becomes, how much more you will enjoy your life, and your consistent ability to be yourself.

Start by taking the element self-survey on the next two pages. This is a quick survey that will establish, for you – at the present time – your relationship to each of the four elements.

It is a Yes/No question: If the statement is true 50% or more of the time, say yes and score 1; if less than 50% of the time, say no and score zero and if undecided, give it a score of ½. This survey is also available online at: DebraSilvermanAstrology.com

Water

1. I cry easily   –
2. I am sentimental (like to save sentimental objects)   –
3. I become non-verbal when upset   –
4. My body gets immediate gut reactions to people   –
5. I second-guess myself   –
6. My self-talk tends to be negative   –
7. I am a private person and I cherish private time   –
8. I can be hypersensitive, emotionally or physically   –
9. I am fascinated by the super-natural   –
10. Music is a necessity in my life   –

TOTAL   –

Air

1. I find words easily and others consider me talkative   –
2. I enjoy watching people and asking questions   –
3. I fill in or finish people's sentences   –
4. I observe and analyze people   –
5. I easily get bored with people and want to move on   –
6. It is easy for me to remember numbers and details   –
7. I am easily distracted by external stimulus   –
8. I change plans/directions easily   –
9. I frequently forget where I put things   –
10. Harmony is essential, even if the cost is high   –

TOTAL   –

Earth

1. Saving money is important to me   _
2. Others consider me to be practical and grounded   _
3. I clean when I am upset   _
4. I am thorough and deliberate when I work   _
5. I love to eat and am sensitive to tastes and smells   _
6. I prefer to be in control   _
7. Being in nature is essential for me   _
8. I am goal-oriented and I get results   _
9. People can rely on me and consider me dependable   _
10. I am slow to change   _

TOTAL _

Fire

1. I thrive on exercise, athletics and expending physical energy   _
2. I am outspoken and frequently say things that get me in trouble   _
3. I have lots of energy and am enthusiastic and passionate   _
4. People would like to turn my volume down or think I'm too intense _
5. It is easy for me to laugh and find the humor in life   _
6. I am deeply into philosophy and/or spirituality   _
7. I inspire others to take action   _
8. People get mad at me – anger can be an issue, either my own or others' _
9. I can be the life of a party   _
10. I fight for the underdog and/or love to argue and debate   _

TOTAL _

Chapter 4

THE STORY OF WATER

"Through love, all pain turns to medicine.
The cure for anything is sweat, tears, or the sea."
—ISAAK DINESEN

This chapter is about the element of water, though it's a story about a firefighter. It's funny, but often men who are water are disguised as another element because it's not easy for them to share their tender watery ways with the world.

Charlie is a handsome guy. For twenty some years, he was a lieutenant in a New York City fire department with a one-truck firehouse (six men on every shift). Over his years with the department he emerged as a fearless firefighter and a leader of men.

Charlie says that he can hardly remember a day when there wasn't some kind of dramatic incident that occurred at his station: fires in trash cans, cats stuck in trees, smoke billowing through a house. He and his team were busy all the time. Then, having stayed in one job for over two decades it was time to retire.

His last day was September 8, 2001. It was a big deal. His brother flew in from Hawaii for the final party, a roast, and he turned his job over to his good friend, Paul Mitchell.

Charlie's dream was to retire in Kauai and transition into a much more mellow lifestyle. So on the morning of September 11, 2001, Charlie and his brother were on a plane leaving New Jersey headed westbound. Shortly into the flight, as they were flying over New York City, lo and behold, from Charlie's side of the plane, he looks out of his window and sees smoke; huge flames and fire bleeding from the World Trade Center. He was miles high in the sky, far away from his firehouse, and his city was on fire. Charlie was frozen in shock.

The plane was forced to land in Ohio. He rented a car and immediately drove back to New York City. It was simple – duty called.

His unit was shattered. The new lieutenant, his friend Paul Mitchell, was killed, and so were too many men to count; hundreds of Charlie's friends were gone.

For the next several months Charlie remained in the city, working at Ground Zero, looking for the remains of his men and friends. He called this "sacred work" as he sought to return evidence of his friends back to their families. It was the only thing he could do.

Water people feel pain as a universal sensation. These are the people who watch the news and cry. It is as if the common denominator of humanity runs through their blood and they ride the waves of the collective sensitivity.

Pain transforms us for good or bad. It takes us deeper into our humanity. We can either open our hearts to feel, or numb out and close down. Both pain and pleasure are emotional doorways that stretch us into vulnerability – a word we know too little about until life demands of us to know it better.

Charlie was sitting dead center in the middle of pain central and could not get away from it. He had to eat the poison of this pain, partly because of the loss of so many friends, and because he was haunted by what had happened. When he came to me for help, his eyes wild with confusion, he kept repeating these questions over and over: "How is it possible that I retired on Sept 8th? How is it possible that I was on the plane on September 11th? Why did Paul go and not me?"

And he cried. His pain tore him open and this big leader of men bawled like a baby, choking on his tears as he spoke. This was the healthy way to be in water, to be with pain and to hold steady. Charlie was doing his work and it wasn't easy. He could have turned his pain into anger. He could have shut down and never let another person love him again. But he didn't do that. He cried, he let the pain touch him and it changed him.

Here are the big questions: How do we surrender to the emotional pain of loss and find wisdom in it? How do we accept the unacceptable? The key word here is surrender.

Charlie couldn't answer the question of why he was spared, why his friends were the ones who had to go down. Sometimes there are no answers – which is difficult for the ego that wants to make up stories so that things make sense and we don't feel pain. Charlie had an ego. He was a powerful man whose job it was to help people, and he was facing his own inability to make sense of what had happened. He had to learn surrender, how to stay open to his feelings, and to not know how to change the crushing cruelty of what had happened. He had to become a student of life and, even more importantly, he had to learn how to forgive the men who killed his friends. Perhaps it is for this reason that he lived to tell the story.

> ...It is as if the common denominator of humanity runs through Water people's blood... they ride the waves of the collective sensitivity.

Forgiveness is a big part of the challenge of water. Over many centuries, there is a huge body of historical pain that contaminates our collective psyche. Our memories will not let us forget the pain of the ancestors, and history then runs through the veins of every generation; Jews hate Arabs, Blacks hate Whites, Catholic resist the Protestant and on and on it goes. Healthy water is learning to heal the pain, to release, to ask for forgiveness and to carry on with a new story.

9/11 changed Charlie. He has become a professional yoga teacher with his own studio. He is part of a large community where he shares his love for life, his sensitivity, and his joy. He told me that he had to make his life even bigger for being allowed to live. He has done just that.

And so I ask you, who do you have to forgive? Who do you need to ask forgiveness from? This is the doorway to emotional wisdom. And it all starts with your ability to forgive yourself and the unforgivable. Clean water is the source of all life.

Chapter 5

WORKING WITH THE ELEMENT OF WATER

Water – the four-step element program

The unconscious mind is ruled by emotions. Water is the emotional doorway of the four elements. Emotions ask you to be aware of your feelings that have been hidden away in your unconscious mind. Bringing them back into objective awareness allows you to release old wounds. It is about understanding and practicing the art of forgiveness, releasing the past (childhood memories) into a new space of healing and acceptance.

Water provides a tremendous capacity to feel. With a memory like an elephant, it can trigger the emotional body to distraction. Water is responsive – its emotional barometer constantly dog-paddling back-and-forth from compassion to pain. At the highest level, Water is Christ energy – it loves and wants to heal everyone and everything. The lower level of Water is excessive empathy that takes on another's pain, and has the possibility of wallowing in it – which can cause depression and lead to infinite therapy, spring-boarding addictions and weight problems.

Water either gets overwhelmed or becomes very good at sitting in stillness. It goes one of two ways. Either you're very gifted at taking care of the negative realm – being able to feel negativity and not getting lost in it – or, you find yourself scaring the crap out of yourself with one bad thought. It goes to extremes. That's what happens with Water. Yin-yang.

Too much Water – you drown in feelings.

THE STEPS

1. **EXPLORE: Go inside and identify the element's energies and patterns in your life.**

2. **ARTICULATE: Put words to your elemental patterns – speak with a trusted witness, laugh about it together.**

3. **INVESTIGATE: Acknowledge the strengths and shadow-sides. Identify and get familiar with your elemental lessons.**

4. **TRANSFORM: Begin a practice to create a new paradigm.**

Not enough water and your emotional body freezes and you are numb, like ice.

Healthy Water is when we learn to feel the pain and own our part in creating it. To release it, to ask for forgiveness, and carry on with a new story. We can learn how to find the emotional wisdom to choose our responses.

Here are the big questions when you *EXPLORE* water:

- How do I surrender to the emotional pain of loss and find wisdom in it?

- How do I accept the unacceptable?

- Can I allow myself to feel and not move away from the awkward sensations of loneliness, sadness, depression?

Take the time to go inside to reflect on your emotions and how you deal with your feelings. What are the habitual thoughts that are reoccurring inside your emotional realm?

> Ask yourself,
> "Where in my body
> am I feeling that?"
> Let the emotions speak,
> if they want to.

If you feel stuck, just ask, "Where am I in pain? What am I feeling?" Next, find it in your body. Ask yourself, "Where in my body am I feeling that?" Sit with it, compassionately, and allow your human nature to be acceptable. Don't feel like you have to let it go; let the emotions have a voice.

Review the elemental survey (water) you completed earlier on: are you in touch with your feelings? If it's a low number, next time you are disrupted or emotionally affected, honor that. Slow down, close your eyes, and take the time to allow feelings to expand by breathing into them. Feelings just need time, awareness, and acceptance.

When you are ready, spend some time journaling your reflections. Journaling is a great way to begin bringing your internal dialogue out and to assist you in identifying what you are feeling. Start with the words, "I feel."

Once you have written about them, explore what patterns and energies are associated with your feelings. You can use the list below if you get stuck. Begin to use the wisdom of the Observer to see your patterns at a distance, as if you are in the audience watching a play. Do you understand the plot? Have you seen this play before? Do you believe you know what is going to happen next? We all repeat patterns over and over again.

Then ask yourself, "What am I scared of?" Write about it, talk about it. The emotional body deserves attention. Ask yourself, "Is the pain personal or collective?" So often what we are feeling is a human experience that is echoed or amplified from all those around us. If you scored high on water you are likely to be a sensitive or empath and not even know the source of your moods and feelings.

> You are likely to be a sensitive and not even know the source of your moods and feelings.

Take it one step further. Read the description of Water people. Reflect again and journal about what else you are now aware of regarding your behaviors and patterns. Remember to turn off the ego – the eternal judge – and turn on your Observer, who doesn't judge and even celebrates your ability to care and feel.

Now ARTICULATE and voice your repetitive emotional content. "I am always worried about money, work, kids, career. There is not enough." Speak with a trusted witness, laugh about it together. Speak of how often you scare yourself. Water people tend to be very private. They do not want to share the deep and hidden parts of their life because they're so emotional, so sensitive and – usually – embarrassed. It is safe for you to open to those who understand emotions and are able to hold your heart, because they don't judge emotions. This is what you long for, to be heard and felt.

WATER people will relate to the following:
- I cry easily
- I am sentimental (I like to save sentimental objects)
- I become non-verbal when upset
- My body gets immediate gut reactions to people
- I worry about the ones I love and/or second-guess myself
- My self-talk tends to be negative
- I am a private person and I cherish private time
- I can be hypersensitive, emotionally or physically
- I am fascinated by the supernatural (mystics attract me)
- Music is a necessity in my life

Water's Energies and Keywords

- Intuition, gut feelings, non-verbal
- Family of origin holds a distracting influence
- Beginning of every cycle we sense, feel with our intuition
- Quiet, introverted
- Mysteries of life, including occult and magic – psychic ability
- Sensuality, love nature and intimacy
- Highly sexual, especially as teenagers
- Healers
- Mother, comfort, home
- Great capacity to feel – tears, emotions
- Childhood fears are bigger for Water kids
- Homebody, likes to save and collect things of sentimental value
- Absorbs negativity; psychic sponges and permeable
- Sacredness, rituals
- Personal space; sacred spaces
- Rules the unconscious – easily influenced, easily hypnotized
- Nurturer – loves to cook
- Poet, visionary, creative dreamer, rich imagination
- The Yum-yum factor – pleasures of senses
- Ecological vision; huge compassion for physical Earth
- Decorator, interior design, great aesthetics
- Strong memories of emotional events
- Feels pain – pain can get "stuck" in their bodies
- Music, meditation, and yoga
- Needs to be able to release
- Reactive, and highly emotional
- Perceptive, intuitive, and receptive
- Sensitive – empathic – cuddly
- Hesitates – doesn't like asking for help
- Recluse, secretive, private
- Rules dreamtime – unconscious
- Changes moods easily
- Energetically sensitive to "vibes" and invisible realm
- Stays in a rut when scared
- Compassion
- Must stay in touch with feelings – sometimes challenging

Strengths of Water

- The ability to be in stillness, to accept pain and pleasure without preference
- The practice of forgiveness and acceptance – having compassion for the perpetrator
- Having intact boundaries, which allows you to say "No" and be guilt-free
- The practice and art of letting go
- Self-care as a priority

Shadow of Water

- Overly protective, and guarded.
- Giving away boundaries, complaining about always giving and never receiving
- Indulging in alcohol, drugs, and sex
- Prone to depression, complaining and wallowing in emotions – which lends itself to addiction
- Fear-ridden with paranoia or phobias
- Hypochondria; they get sick a lot, because their emotions show up as symptoms in the body
- Fear of dying and fear of loss
- Negative and limiting beliefs – addicted to limitations
- Family issues never resolved, holding onto past wounds and carrying them into the present.
- Projecting their own faults onto others because they can't see outside their compelling emotional experience
- Lack of impulse control. Reactive and overly sensitive
- Can get distracted by spiritual matters that take them off-planet

To *INVESTIGATE* your emotional lessons, take the attitude of a student; reflect on your life; ask questions; explore your habitual patterns and habits. Your elemental lessons continually show up asking you to sit in the Observer and learn something new. Sometimes it is a quiet nudge, or it's a shout in your subconscious, a two-by-four hitting you, yelling, "Wake up!"

Learn to use the Observer and ask for what you need. Beware of your need to please and shape-shift like a chameleon, taking on qualities of those around you. Practice saying, "Yes" to your soul and receiving from others. Equally important is to say, "No" and be guilt-free. It is okay for you to come first.

Get familiar with the strength of Water and its shadow. Reflect and speak about these qualities.

The trick to getting healthy water is not allowing your emotions to get backed up: release / express what you feel inside. It's okay to cry, to get angry. Don't overindulge in the pity-party realm for too long. Alcoholism, sexual, and fear-based addictions may result when the emotional body harbors pain and has no means for release. (AA is full of Water and Fire people.) Find a positive, constructive means to release your emotions.

Make sure you don't take on other people's pain. When you lose your boundaries, don't complain you're always giving and not getting. Stop that! Just sit with others, hold their hand and let them feel. Clean, clear water promotes healing. The wisdom of Water is to allow others to own their pain, without trying to fix it, simply to allow the individual to marinate in the depths of sadness, despair, or grief with gentleness and acceptance. It is healthy to be sad. But if someone is overindulging in their pain, and not able to get over it in appropriate time, then there are side effects that prevent joy and are the source of depression, negativity, and moodiness.

Anger is an emotion that hides sadness. For some people, they go to anger while others go to sadness. In both cases this is a healthy reaction that requires attention and acceptance. It's okay to be sad or angry if you are in your Observer.

As you begin to honor your emotions, you will develop compassion for human nature. One gentle way to release old patterns is to give yourself a sense of permission simply to be "human." Start by reading the list of permissions below and choose one or two.

Permissions for Water

- I will allow myself to feel and listen deeply. My soul longs for quiet.
- It is okay to be alone. I will give myself time off, guilt-free, to enjoy my retreat time.
- I know when to stop swimming in my sensitivity. It is important for

> As you begin to honor your emotions, you will develop compassion for human nature.

me to maintain healthy emotional boundaries with others and develop emotional maturity. Sometimes I must simply neglect my distracting sensitivity.

- I will allow myself to celebrate my sensitivity as a gift and not a curse.
- It is totally okay to be quiet and comfortable. I don't have to talk. It's okay to avoid parties. I am allowed to value my quiet.
- I will be grateful and acknowledge how blessed I am.
- I will allow myself positive time to read, meditate, watch TV, and take naps.
- I will listen to my own truth, by being still and paying attention to my body.
- It is my pleasure to meditate, pray, do yoga.
- I am really good at love, care-taking and kindness, especially with children and animals. These are my specialties.

Now it is time to *TRANSFORM* by creating a new paradigm. You might:

- Learn how to deal with sensitivity and release the past (childhood memories) to be here now. This may require a good therapist, or spending time in your inner world with an intention to heal.
- Learn and practice the art of forgiveness and acceptance. Pray for help.
- Listen to the language of symbols, dreams, and intuition to make the unconscious conscious. Water has the most developed capacity for psychic phenomena, reading minds, and healing.
- Develop boundaries. Water absorbs what is around it, so one needs to know how to clean off the emotions and psychic fields of other people. Smudging, incense, candles, music are all ways to clean up your space.

The right use of Water is knowing how and when to release and forgive the past. Clean Water is a spiritual depth that allows us to have faith that there is a reason for everything, even when it is hard to believe it's true. Having healthy Water means we have learned to heal the pain, to release, to ask forgiveness, and carry on with a new story. Now, we're able to feel our feelings, and process them in real time.

To bring the element of Water into balance or create a practice to maintain clear, healthy Water, here are some suggestions to get you started.

Meditation

Learning meditation is the short answer to the question of how to cultivate Water's emotional stability. Using your breath, take the pain up from the belly and down your back/spine and into the cord connecting down into Mother Earth.

Allow yourself to find the voice inside your head that says, "I am safe. I am protected. I am provided for." Let these words float through your head and continue to take deep breaths. Repeat over and over again. Act as if it *IS* true. Soon you will feel the safety of your soul's presence.

Connect with Your Feelings and Let Your Emotions Flow

Avoid hiding from your vulnerability and tender parts. You might try journaling each day, reflecting on something that touched your heart that day. Get a little courageous and begin sharing those experiences with someone. A word of caution – it's important to cry. If you have clinical depression in your family and your emotional realm seems out of control, there is no shame in asking for help; antidepressants really do work and you will know if you need them by deeply listening to your body.

Create a Sacred Space and Get Comfortable with Silence

Create or find a sacred place. Maybe it is a quiet path in the woods or a corner of your bedroom where you can be with yourself and touch the tender places inside of you. Then each day carve out time to be alone.

Everyone can find ten minutes each day to be still and reconnect with themselves. Use this time as silent nourishment for your heart.

Reflect on Your Patterns – Observe and Breathe

Remember your response to Chapter 4, The Story of Water. The first step is to observe, and see your patterns and behaviors. List them, share them, forgive yourself, forgive the other, laugh at them and then let them go. Then come up with a handful of people – your personal dream team – with whom you can be raw and clumsy. Invite them to be your mirror to reflect and investigate with you the pattern from a neutral non-judgmental place. Once you identify your patterns, agree to pause and breathe next time you begin to repeat your emotional triggers. This gives your Observer a chance to show up. Think, pause, breathe, and receive new wisdom.

I have a client whose husband died, and for years she complained of sadness. One day I said, "Let's call your sadness with your husband's name," and when it would appear, she'd say, "Oh, Henry is here again," and it would soften her sadness into tenderness and into an open heart. It's okay to be sad.

When the Going Gets Tough – Laugh

You know your Observer is working when you are able to laugh at yourself and the situations that trigger you. Humor is the result of looking at your humanity from a distance. We are all a bit crazy and funny. And laughter is the healing balm for all of us.

Chapter 6

WATER WOMEN

To most people I appear to be completely confident. Actually, I have low self-esteem that I am careful to keep well hidden. The truth is, I am often judging myself harshly; I tend to think that my work could be better, and that I am not attractive. Others say that I am talented and good looking, but I cannot receive their complements; I dwell on my deficiencies. Health and well-being are daily concerns; I worry about illness and money, and I wish that I had more self-discipline. When I am emotional, I will either stop eating completely, or alternately binge on my favorite comfort foods.

When I feel depressed or angry, I can become extremely agitated. I might scream and cry for no apparent reason. I struggle to control myself and generally, I succeed. When I fail to contain my emotions, the result is embarrassment. Rarely do I lose control in public; only my family and some close friends know how emotional I can get.

My intense feelings color my world. I can't pretend to be happy when I'm not. I often need help to alter my mood during the day with coffee, tea, or something soothing. This allows me to relieve the pressure of my sensitivity. Music is essential for me; classical or something soft speaks to my soul and has an incredibly calming affect. Being outside is the easiest way for me to forget about my problems. It can be as simple as a walk around the park; it doesn't have to be an expedition. Flowers and streams, colorful gardens, the ocean, these are the places where I like to spend time. Horses and cats, and animals of all kinds fascinate me; everything has a consciousness.

Social

I have an immediate, strong, gut impression of people that I meet. I either like the person or I do not. I am seldom ambivalent, and the feelings that I get from people often turn out to be correct. I believe that I can see deeply into them. On the one hand, it is a gift to be so perceptive; on the other hand, it is a challenge to use the information that I receive responsibly. I can be impatient with people and they occasionally annoy me. I wish that I were less judgmental.

I am comfortable being alone, especially in nature. I like to unwind and relax without too much talking. When I am with my partner, we communicate through silence. Body language to me is just as important as talking. I can tell a lot about someone by how they look and move. If I am in a long conversation, I can lose myself; people easily influence me. I want to communicate what I am feeling, but I do not always have the words to express myself. I am happiest when I am busy and my mind is clear of thoughts.

I willingly give the energy required to support long-term friendships. I choose my friends carefully and nurture my relationships because my friends are as important to me as my family. I am very impressionable. In social situations, I instinctively respond to a person's essence. If I decide that they are not authentic, I will leave immediately. I will not socialize without a time limit. I must have the keys to my car handy and the door clearly in sight or else I feel trapped.

Relationships

My relationships endure because of my complete commitment to love. I consider it my duty to make sacrifices that will make my partner happy. I am a sensitive and considerate lover. I prefer deeply involving experiences rather than superficial, sensual encounters. Tenderness provides me with needed emotional sustenance. When there is conflict or disagreement, I will consciously avoid entanglement; direct confrontation is not one of my strengths. I am often analyzing my relationships, trying to determine what childhood dynamic set a particular behavior in motion. My desire is that we all open our hearts and speak the truth with love and kindness. Psychology and relationship are continuing interests, as are ritual and spirituality.

When my relationship is not working, I am reluctant to complain. I tend to be secretive about disappointments. My innate stubbornness can prevent me from expressing myself. Only when the relationship approaches meltdown will I grudgingly reveal my inner feelings. Actually, displays of emotion are distasteful for me. I cry much too easily, which is humiliating and only sends me deeper into myself where I can be very self-critical. When the problem becomes overwhelming, I willingly seek therapy or a mentor who can help solve my problems.

I can be a quiet person, although when I am relaxed and calm I can be quite talkative. I only open to a few select people. To some, it may appear that I am shy, but in truth, I am only reserved. I am cautious and defensive until I feel comfortable with someone, especially with men. The men I like are sensitive and caring; I know that they will be patient with me. Spending quality time with my partner is essential. Once I consider you my friend, it is easy for me to reveal my feelings.

I am a sensitive, private, deeply emotional person who only wants to be close to those I love and believe that they will be there for me when I am in need. Will you understand me?

Family

My parents and family members occupy center stage in my life. Family responsibilities are a priority; my home is always open to those I love. I am glad to play the host; I am considerate and warm. I enjoy entertaining loved ones, cooking and providing a warm supportive home life. It is a pleasure to serve those I love and I am always looking for ways to bring people closer.

I love animals and children. I dream about volunteering at all kinds of places, but I am often too busy helping others and then I feel guilty. I often feel I am not doing enough.

Work

At work, I am responsible, determined, and conscientious. Leadership comes naturally to me; my colleagues respect my ability to combine gentle humanity with high productivity. I shine when it comes to creativity; it is my most outstanding feature. Whether it is music, art, or literature, inspiration will find me and I will excel. I am happiest when I am working with my hands or being creative. My work ethic insists that I try to do my work independently; to ask for help is embarrassing and I avoid it. Completely absorbed by the task at hand, I will continue working much longer than I should. Only when I am exhausted will I consider rest and recuperation. In order to regenerate, I must have time to be alone, away from everyone except for a few friends or family.

I do love to assist my family. Too often I give myself away. As I get older and I learn to value myself, my whole life changes. My lesson is learning to ask for help and making me a priority.

Chapter 7

WATER MEN

I am a soulful person; I like situations that are deep and rich. People call me dreamy and often ask me what planet I am on. Friends say that I am distant and self-absorbed. This surprises me, although I know that I am frequently introspective. I do not mean to offend anyone or reject them – it's just that my inner world is so consuming that I am often distracted. I call it communing with the soul. It is my way of finding solace in an over-stimulated world. A close relationship with Spirit is natural for me because I am willing to be still and wait for the inspiration.

Beauty connects me directly to spirit. Color, form, and grace move me deeply and profoundly. When my soul is at peace I can see the beauty all around me. When my personality is calm, I can flow through life. Being calm and at peace is my ultimate desire; to be in tune with life is my aspiration. When I am centered within myself, colors appear brighter, the sun is warmer, and the presence of Spirit is everywhere.

I have always loved rituals and I know how to reach deep inside myself to find sacred places. Early in the morning, my soul is most open and alert. I need to preserve these quiet hours for introspection. Music is always inspiring, especially while I cook. I am a domestic person and spending time at home rejuvenates me. A quiet evening watching TV or reading a book in front of the fire is pure bliss. Creating a comfortable space at work or at home is one of my pleasures. I get a sense of security from personalizing my environment.

When I am stressed, my nature is to keep my feelings inside; even at the best of times I find it hard to verbalize. When I was young, I was far more sensitive than the other guys. It has always been hard for me to hold back the tears, and there have been times when I have questioned my manhood.

I long to be understood, although I often wish it could happen beyond words. My art, my dreams, and my generous heart ought to be enough. If only the world was softer, kinder, and men could be feminine without that challenging our manhood. I would be a lot happier.

Social

I am an intensely private person although I do have a few close friends. While I do not open myself to many people, those that I do let in are deeply and unconditionally loved. I have a place in society and I contribute my unique viewpoint for the betterment of all. I am an artist, a writer, a dreamer, and a humanitarian. I help people find the beauty in their lives. Mysticism and spirituality are my contributions. Without me as a member of society, art and the inner world would be neglected.

I am not good at chitchat. I find socializing difficult and I would prefer just to be with my family, wife, or close friends. Large crowds make me nervous and I avoid them. The presence of so many individuals rocks my stability and it takes persistence to keep myself centered. I am so sensitive to people it is as though I can see right through them. I often have first impressions that are so strong that I have trouble maintaining my objectivity. Frequently it is painfully obvious to me what people are thinking and feeling, and I wonder if they are aware of how transparent they are. When I share what I see in other people, I sound judgmental. As a result, I am usually guarded about my opinions of people. At my worst, I can be judgmental when I attach values to my perceptions. At my best, I can help people see themselves in a new way through my eyes. I am a natural psychologist.

As an adult, I cope with my sensitivity by maintaining a distance from people. As a child, I believed that I was different from the other children, an odd duck, and I had trouble fitting in. I was tagged as a loner when I was in high school, and some of the kids called me conceited. The rumor was that I thought I was better than everyone else. As a teenager I was often overwhelmed in social situations, being sensitive to so many was exhausting.

Relationships

I am a very sexual/sensual man. Sex is one way that I touch my spirituality. My sensitivity applies doubly to my lovemaking. It allows me to be open and vulnerable. I am a committed lover, but when I have been rejected, even gently, it is enough to take away my drive. I am too sensitive to be assertive after a rejection, and it is even more difficult after rejection to verbalize my hurt feelings. This is an area that I do not wish to talk about. Please don't interpret my quiet for not caring. I care so much it is hard for me to talk about it. I care about humanity, my family, and my soul. I am deep, spiritual, and psychological. Be gentle with me and I will open.

I love children and my closest pet. Don't misinterpret my sometimes ice-like qualities as though I don't care. I care so much I go numb to protect my emotional body. If you can just be quiet with me and ask me a few questions I will open. Silence is the doorway to my opening.

Family

My family is my main source of personal contact; often this puts extra pressure on my wife and children to provide the intimacy that I need. Sometimes I feel like I lose myself because I put the needs of the family before my own. I love my kids so much that I can sacrifice my own well-being to attend to their needs. I would do anything for them; they are so very important to me. Just thinking about them can bring tears to my eyes. At times, it seems they take advantage because I am so passive and agreeable. I tend to be a workaholic, and after a week of work and the demands at home, I hardly have any time for me.

As much as I love my family, silly things can annoy me. Especially when I am emotional. The messy room, bad table manners, the whining voice can affect me as though they were personal insults. If I overreact and I become emotional, it is very embarrassing and I feel that I have failed to be a loving, tolerant parent. It is difficult for me to apologize when I lose emotional control; the humiliation makes me want to withdraw into myself until the feeling goes. Some say that I can easily let myself drift into denial.

Work

In the workplace, I find that I can easily lose myself in the job at hand, relieving me of life's worries. I prefer to work by myself, but if I must work with others I am able to do so without being drawn into unnecessary politics. At work, people rely on me for counsel; they tell me their problems and usually I can soothe them and provide wisdom. It is easy for me to listen to my colleagues' problems, although I rarely, if ever, disclose my own feelings. My boss says that I am a good judge of character and can usually tell whether someone is telling the truth or not.

I have many creative, sometimes radical ideas. I have often been accused of being obsessive or impractical. Negative comments divert my creative flow and hurt my feelings. I know how to do my professional work with proficiency and timeliness, but when it comes to my personal life, I am not as effective. There is an obvious discrepancy between my personal life and the power and clarity that I express at work. I am inclined to overwork, and with the demands of home and family, I hardly have any time for me.

Chapter 8

THE STORY OF AIR

This is the story of four angels that came in different sizes and colors. A black 6'2" man from Watts, and three white ladies who came together to do their magic. Kenny spent twenty-seven years in San Quentin with a life sentence for kidnapping and robbery. The four angels – who didn't all know each other – were drawn to a friendship with him out of pure synchronicity and a sincere desire to help. I consider Kenny one of my dearest friends.

"My parents split," Kenny Fairley told me during a visit with him at San Quentin prison. "My mother was having different boyfriends. On August 29, my father got murdered, stabbed to death coming out of a liquor store where he had gone to cash his Social Security check. It was a little bit after the Watts riots. I was thirteen or fourteen. It was the saddest thing that happened in my life around that time.

"In 11th grade," he continued, "I was heavily into experimenting with drugs. I was smoking marijuana and PCP. I was on the verge of being out of control. I felt as though my number was coming. I was caught in a kidnap and robbery. This woman was turning right on a freeway ramp – I jumped into her car, told her where to turn, took her money and took off running. I was given a life sentence for a crime that was worthy of seven years at the most."

I met Kenny through an unusual series of events. When my son was one year old, I hired a nanny named Ammi. One of Ammi's good friends, Helena, worked at San Quentin as a volunteer. She was leaving California and called to ask Ammi to be Kenny's pen pal. Helena told us this guy Kenny was special and she hated to desert him. Being the saint that Ammi is, she readily agreed. (Kenny later nicknamed her "the Quintessa of Love.")

Ammi and I both began writing Kenny. We sent monthly care packages to him – all conforming to strict prison rules – filled with Oreo cookies, canned sardines, crackers, and other things he could not get in prison. Intrigued by our correspondence, we went to San Quentin to meet him.

Kenny grew up in Watts in the 1960s. He was busted in his early twenties and given bad legal advice. He unknowingly took a plea deal and was sentenced to life. Kenny did commit a crime, but he didn't hurt anyone. Because he was black and poor, they threw him away with a life sentence.

Let's consider the element of Air. Air people love freedom. They think outside the box. Kenny lost his freedom and his ability to make decisions. Friendships happen in magical ways. Air people have a way of blending and crossing boundaries. They are color-blind and are gifted to see without judgment. For air people, we're all sharing the same air and, therefore, we're all friends.

> Air people have a way of blending and crossing boundaries. They are gifted to see without judgment. For air people, we're all sharing the same air and, therefore, we're all friends.

Friendships and relationships are holy for Air people. They love to be in communication and close. Kenny and I wrote to each other every week for years and years.

Kenny has a wonderful sense of humor, and everything made him laugh. He made up words and nicknames for things. His nicknames for me continue to be, "Debbie-Deb" and "My lady of magic." For all he'd been through, he never lost the smile on his face.

Year after year, I visited. Every Monday morning for eleven years, I sent a card to him. Kenny continued to confide in me, "I have this feeling I'm going to get out." My message was always the same: "Don't give up." I lost count how many of those spiritual cards with rainbows and sparkling positive messages I bought for him. One day, I was telling this story to a wealthy client and she remarked, "Why don't you get him the best lawyer in California, and I'll pay for it?"

I couldn't believe it. I was so excited. For so many years, I'd been telling Kenny, "Don't give up," but secretly feeling, "I'm so full of it, giving him false hope." Suddenly, the dream seemed possible.

Kenny found a lawyer in Sacramento that he'd heard about through the prison grapevine: Steven Sanders. When Sanders opened up the case file, he said, "This is ridiculous! This is absolutely wrong! What is he doing in there? Twenty-seven years is outrageous!" Up to this point, Kenny had attended seventeen parole hearings, none of which ever amounted to anything more than a ten-minute conversation with parole officers who would not make eye contact.

But this parole hearing was different. Sanders educated Kenny about how to present himself. About an hour into the meeting, there was a consensus that Kenny had been sentenced unjustly. Then, when they looked at Kenny's psychiatric report, they saw that it had the wrong name on it.

"We'd let him out now," the authorities agreed, "but we need a new psychiatric report first." It took six months to get another report, because that's how the system is. It took another half-year to get through all the red tape, and finally Kenny was freed.

He was released within hours of President Obama's receiving his nomination for presidency, the same day forty-five years earlier Martin Luther King made his famous "I Have a Dream" speech. Synchronicity is a specialty of Air people; their timing is a sequence of magical events that occurs far beyond reason, gifting them with a unique sense of magic. He was let off parole on this same day in 2013 – five years later.

Now, take a deep breath. The story isn't over yet.

This entire process was fraught with tension and governmental snafus. (Time now for a little bit of Air: "Snafu" is an army word. It is an acronym for "Situation Normal All F***ed Up." Now back to Kenny's story….)

> Synchronicity is a specialty of Air people; their timing is a sequence of magical events that occurs far beyond reason, gifting them with a unique sense of magic.

My dream was to document Kenny's story. I wanted to film the moment he got off the bus. He was to be released in Lancaster, California, near his sister's home, which is an hour outside of LA. I managed to raise enough money to make a ten-minute documentary of Kenny's release. I arrived in Los Angeles for this momentous event, only to discover that the prison authorities had postponed his release date for seven days… and had not informed anyone – not Kenny's family, not me. We only learned of the change when I called to arrange to pick him up.

I flew back home to Colorado, and a week later I returned to L.A. While driving down the highway with Tamara, the camerawoman, I got a call from Kenny's sister, Sheila. "You aren't going to like this," she said. I immediately thought, *Oh, no, we missed his arrival time, and we won't be able to shoot that first moment!*

"The parole officer just called to say Kenny's release is delayed, again," she reported. "Probably until Tuesday." Today was Thursday. I had just flown in for a second time, and was now being told it was delayed. Unfortunately, I couldn't wait another five days.

"Give me the phone number!" I demanded. I called; after many rings, a female parole officer finally answered. She confirmed that Kenny would not be released until the following week. I was furious, speechless – not a common occurrence for any Air personality (which I am).

"You ought to be happy he's getting out at all," Ms. Parole Officer smirked into the receiver. "He's a lifer." Thinking of Kenny and his infinite patience, I kept my cool. We decided to keep driving to his sister Sheila's house and say "Hi," before going back to Los Angeles to wait – *again*. Tamara went home to L.A. to be with her family. For some reason, I decided to stay with Sheila, and rent a car the next day to get back to L.A.

Suddenly, the phone rang. It was the parole officer. Kenny could be picked up at the Lancaster Office in twenty minutes! We hollered, and shouted, and called Sheila on her cell phone. "We will meet you at the parole office!" I called Tamara, who was already halfway to L.A. "Come back! Kenny's getting out right now, and we need to be there to film it!" We met Kenny as he stepped off the bus – a free man.

He was wearing a gray sweat suit, cheap running shoes, and carrying a small box containing all my cards, his paperwork, personal items, and $200 "get out of jail" cash. He looked like a deer in the headlights as the authorities unshackled his wrists and ankles after a miserable seven-hour bus ride from San Quentin. Turns out that prison officials purposely make an inmate's release data vague in case some gang member or criminal element is seeking revenge and learns about the particulars. Or maybe it's just one last little bit of torture?

We jumped out of the car, everybody cheering, and hugging Kenny like he was a football star who had just made the winning touchdown. It was time for us to head home to celebrate.

It was Thursday night, August 28, 2008 – a date I'll never forget. We returned to Sheila's house, greeted by the sweet, smoky aroma of barbecue ribs – Kenny's favorite. Sheila had begun preparations the day before, browning the ribs, putting them in a slow cooker with molasses and her special secret ingredients.

The first thing that Kenny did when we arrived at Sheila's was fall to his knees and kiss the ground. "Wow, real grass," he exclaimed, still kneeling down and rubbing the live, emerald carpet with his massive, but gentle, hands. "There wasn't no grass where I was at, man. No trees."

The next morning, we dined at IHOP where Kenny marveled at the pancakes. "These pancakes are steaming hot, man!" He stared at the golden cakes as the butter melted. "I haven't seen butter melt like that in years!" he admired, filling his mouth with a forkful of manna. After breakfast, we had a marathon shopping expedition. We bought lots of necessities, including a bed. Testing the bed and evaluating our purchase, he beamed, "Wow. I can stretch out! My prison bed was so short I could never stretch out."

"… *for twenty-seven years*," I thought to myself.

There were many, many firsts that week. Every night, Kenny indulged in a hot, leisurely bath. He had only been allowed sporadic cold showers in prison. He wanted fresh fruit. He wanted to taste oysters. He was excited to wake up in the morning and make his own breakfast.

I cried all the way back home to Colorado, unlike my friend Kenny, who didn't shed a tear. This is a trait of Air people; they are detached and can even become numb.

One of Kenny's favorite lines is, "Debbie-Deb, I laugh, because otherwise I'd cry." During twenty-seven years in prison he only cried once – on the day his mom died.

Recently, Kenny was asked how he survived his long incarceration. "By having faith and keeping my heart open to new ideas, and talking and listening to different people, different perspectives. That gave me hope. That, and believing in angels."

Kenny and I have maintained a very close friendship. We are family. Life has a way of connecting souls far beyond our mind's understanding. There are some people you can't get rid of. I am so glad Kenny is a part of my family.

> Life has a way of connecting souls far beyond our mind's understanding.

I visited Kenny in L.A. some months after his release. He and I were driving in the car listening to a Sanskrit chant playing over and over again.

"What kind of music is this?" Kenny asked, puzzled.

"It's called chanting. People use it to remove the chatter out of their heads."

"Oh, like when I would go into my cell and concentrate on my breathing and not think?"

"Yeah, Kenny that's exactly right."

Chapter 9

WORKING WITH THE ELEMENT OF AIR

Air – the four-step element program

Air is the curious mind trying to figure things out. It is the thinker with a powerful desire to know and understand. The essence of Air urges you to share your ideas, ask questions, and find someone to talk to. Air tells stories and uses language to get their point across. The challenge of Air is to notice how set ideas either limit or enhance our ability to feel bonded or separated. Ideas can be as wide as the sky is open, or so small they put you in a box, never to be let out. This is the part of us that thinks we know what is right, according to our point of view, and define ourselves as either liberal or conservative without knowing how to cross the lines.

The Air element devours all sources of information and can spend countless hours listening to television news shows, reading, searching the web and talking about everything and nothing – and eventually ending up confused. Since the beginning of written language, the mind and intellect has assumed the position of power and so for ages has been valued over the heart. From intellects to oracles, to universities, to books, radio and TV personalities, words and language saturate the human psyche. Words have been used in different languages and dialects, systems of thought that describe religions fueling wars. Air can connect us or separate us.

> **THE STEPS**
>
> 1. **EXPLORE: Go inside and identify the element's energies and patterns in your life.**
>
> 2. **ARTICULATE: Put words to your elemental patterns – speak with a trusted witness, laugh about it together.**
>
> 3. **INVESTIGATE: Acknowledge the strengths and shadow-sides. Identify and get familiar with your elemental lessons.**
>
> 4. **TRANSFORM: Begin a practice to create a new paradigm.**

Although Air moves freely, there seems to be an imaginary line which is drawn just above your shoulders – so you can live in your head and never venture down to your heart. Recent scientific studies reveal that the heart is hard-wired to the brain, and the heart itself is comprised largely of neural tissues. In fact, it now appears that the brain is the seat of intellect while the heart is the seat of wisdom!

Air can be a little hard to contain or predict. At times it may be as gentle as a summer breeze, or have the force of a tornado. Change is their constant and variations on a theme are their specialty.

> Air can be a little hard to contain or predict. At times it may be as gentle as a summer breeze, or have the force of a tornado.

If you resonate with the element of Air you might feel self-conscious about this unpredictability. This is where the term "airhead" comes from. You see, Air often comes off as completely confused. They think they are flaky (and sometimes they are), and might appear flaky even if they're not. Their minds go in many directions at the same time. Air, like the wind, can change direction easily – and therefore the energy of this element is that of distraction and spontaneity.

Too much Air – you run the risk of over-valuing the mind and intellect with little connection to your heart. You might forget where you put things and speak out of both sides of your mouth or have a hard time making decisions.

Too little Air – you find yourself lost in your mind and feel unable to get your thoughts out. Too little air might limit your speaking or truth-telling. You might lose interest in people.

We have cultivated, healthy Air when we know how to give weight to words, and not just talk from the head but from the heart.

Here are the big questions when you *EXPLORE* Air:

- How do we honestly express our thoughts and words?
- How do we become aware of the negative thoughts in our intellect to short-circuit the traps our minds fall into?
- Can I accept my airhead qualities without judgment and find them endearing?

Spend time investigating the habitual patterns of Air that are part of your life story. Begin to identify the core beliefs

> Know how to give weight to words, and not just talk from the head but from the heart.

and stories you repetitively tell yourself. How are they serving you in the present moment, or are they? Notice the places where your mind and the words you use to describe yourself have trapped you and have become your inner critic. If you feel stuck, try asking yourself, "What are the first words that come to mind when I describe myself?" List those words and observe the storyline they create. Journal about it. Read out loud what you have written – or have a trusted friend read it to you – and attempt to listen through your heart, not your mind, with compassion.

Review the elemental survey (air) you completed earlier on: to what degree are you aware of how you use your mind and words? Whether you scored low or high, take some time to list the ways you use communication every day.

Begin to use the wisdom of the Observer to see your patterns. Then ask yourself, "How are my thoughts imprisoning me?" Often where you feel trapped is where your mind is being used by your ego to keep the old story running. Your mind gathers evidence, proves and justifies your stories. And he who tells the story tells it best.

Take it one step further. Read the description of Air people. Consider and then journal about what else you are now aware of about your behaviors and patterns. Remember to turn off the ego, turn on the Observer, which is your compassion.

AIR PEOPLE will relate to the following:

- I find words easily and others consider me conversational
- I enjoy watching people and asking questions
- I fill in or finish people's sentences
- I observe and analyze people
- I easily get bored with people and I am always looking for new people to interact with
- It is easy for me to remember numbers and details
- I am easily distracted by external stimulus
- I change plans/direction easily
- I frequently forget where I put things
- Harmony is essential, even if the cost is high

Air Energies and Key Words

- Verbalize, talk, interrupt
- Mediators, lawyers, negotiators, therapists, coaches
- Articulating and writing is easy
- Mind, intellect, school
- Reading is a passion
- Break the rules
- Speed freaks, hate waiting in line
- Keen observation, spectator
- Charming, pleaser personality – politician – schmoozer, can work the room
- Not connected to their emotions – detached, may disappear, evaporate suddenly – unpredictable
- Mathematical, good with numbers (but never thinks so)
- Auditory – nosy – gossip
- Loves people and avoids conflict
- Curious – always studying, reading
- Provokes and stimulates new thoughts
- Loves conversation
- Visionaries – ahead of their time
- Mindful – perky, awake – aware
- Out-of-the-box
- Research and modern science
- Reads anything, and reads a lot
- Insatiable mind
- Can learn to be a great listener
- Comforted by books – libraries – bookstores – amazon.com
- Flaky, forgetful "airhead"
- Telephone, texting, email, computers, technology geeks
- Spontaneous, averse to repetition / mundane; doesn't like plans
- Forgets where they put things
- Messy, scattered, unorganized yet they love organizational tools (but can't find them when they need them)
- Collects Hallmark cards, stationery, books and magazines
- Lighthearted, witty, tickle people with their wit and humor
- Photographic memory

Strengths of Air

- The ability to free-associate and be an idea factory
- To know when not to talk, be in stillness; listen deeply
- To use words to bless and heal, rather than to puncture, hurt, and gossip
- The gift to speak to the unspeakable
- Understand and prioritize relationships
- The fascination of being close to another and seeking harmony
- The awareness of how to be gracious, inclusive and to let others have their own ideas.
- Charming and socially graceful

Shadow of Air

- Co-dependent; dislikes being alone
- Obsessed by being free and spontaneous, unrestrained; may have no respect for others' timetable
- Lacks impulse control, undisciplined; dislikes following the rules
- Remains busy and on the go in order to escape emotional confrontations
- Lies by omitting facts – doesn't tell the whole truth
- Very flirtatious, even if only in their head; feels guilty for being a flirt
- An "idea factory" with no practical application, often dabbling in many things and mastering none
- Dreamers who don't manifest because they don't have a game plan
- All talk and theory, nothing concrete, reads just enough to get the gist and pretends to know all

Now *ARTICULATE* and voice your patterns. Place your hand gently on your heart as you speak. Speaking through your heart is a beginning practice of ensuring your words match your truth.

To *INVESTIGATE* and encourage air, take the attitude of an apprentice: take a class, read a book, join a discussion group to keep your mind active and balanced. To boost your understanding, pick up a book or join a discussion

> Reaching out and asking for contact is an important part of keeping Air alive and vibrant.

group where you have to say or read each word with a beginner's mind.

Learn to use the Observer to watch your mind. This is one of the most powerful practices of the four elements. Get familiar with the strength of Air and its shadow. Does your mind judge and then project your judgments onto others?

The key to clean Air is to have the mind speak through the heart, in the present moment, and in a way that is authentic and honest. It is OK to be direct and blunt as long as the words are not judgmental or filled with projections. Words have power and can be used as daggers to hurt or push people away. Likewise, when you find yourself standing in silence on the sidelines, notice: are you choosing to be on the outside or are you actually hurting and longing for contact? Reaching out and asking for contact is an important part of keeping Air alive and vibrant. Air is the soft, gentle breeze that can tenderly open a heart.

A positive mental attitude supported by affirmations will achieve success in anything. Positive self-talk or inner dialogue sources your manifestation. We are continually affirming subconsciously with our words and thoughts. One gentle way to release your old patterns is to give yourself new permissions. Start by reading the following list of Permissions for Air and choose one or two sentences.

Permissions for Air

- I will learn to talk from the heart, less is more, so as to not get lost in words.
- I will ask myself, "Why are you telling this story? Whom are you serving?"
- I will practice saying these sentences: "I need you." "I miss you." "I feel sad." "I was wrong." "I need help."
- I will agree to disagree. I know disharmony can be healthy.
- I will seek counsel from others and then return to my own knowing.
- I will trust my intuition even if my mind argues.

- Listening means I will stop filling in people's sentences. I will take a deep breath when I need to slow down.
- I acknowledge I am an intellectual person. Even though there is more to learn, I will stop underestimating my mental capacity.
- I will speak to the unspeakable. Speak in first person and avoid kind of's, sort of's and almost.
- I will speak my truth. When I am feeling negative, I will own it; when I am happy, I will own it. I will not gloss over my negative feelings and emotions.

Now it is time to *TRANSFORM* by creating a new paradigm.

> Start a love aff–Air with Y–O–U, and enjoy your own company.

- Start a love aff–Air with y–o–u, and enjoy your own company.
- Take a class – like learning the art of public speaking and social etiquette.
- Find ways to remain and act interested, and engage in the stories of people around you. The personality of air loves to talk while the soul of air loves to listen. Cultivate both in your life.
- Use journaling to establish your own voice. Read what you write out loud to yourself as a form of medicine, so you can hear your own thoughts and feelings. Too many journals are left on the shelf.
- Ask questions – the single most powerful gift that an Air person has is that of knowing how to ask questions not only of others, but also of themselves.
- Let others give you feedback and then listen. Those around you might have had a hard time getting their words into your conversation.
- Find a good listener, coach, therapist, to whom you can talk and talk without censorship. Think of this time as "Air conditioning," getting out the negative is just as important as the positive.

The right use of Air is an innocent mind open to possibilities, and subservient to the direction of the divine. Just as the personality should be in service to the soul, the mind should be in service to the heart – not the other way around.

When you see evolution in the big picture, you are no longer judging destruction and creation, life and death; instead, your mind is big enough to include a humbled posture that reminds you that you are merely a servant to the creative intelligence.

If you wish to bring the element of Air into balance, here are some suggestions.

Meditation

Learning to use mantras in meditation is a short answer to the question of how to tame the mind and cultivate Air. Using your breath to fill each cell in the body with clean air, knowing that each breath of air has escalated from another, helps to remind us how connected we are to each other.

Find time each hour to return to the rhythmic pattern of the breath by taking a few deep breaths, which helps you return to the here and now.

Connect Your Mind to Your Heart

Avoid using your mind and intellect to hide from your vulnerability and tender parts.

You might start by including emotions as you journal each day. Begin your journal with the sentence "I feel…" and then fill in the blanks.

Speak from your heart – this is often known as the practice of courageous conversations. Start with your own voice talking to yourself.

Spend Time Each Day with Awareness

Cultivate your ability to watch your busy mind. It may not be easy to get your internal dialogue to stop. That is not the goal. It is simply to have your Observer on. Perhaps it is walking each evening at the end of your workday, or having time alone in a cozy chair in your home, consciously watching your mind. Cultivating Air includes getting comfortable with being by yourself, listening with compassion to all those voices in your head.

Reflect on Your Patterns – Pause, Breathe, Receive and Believe

Remember your response to the Story of Kenny. Consider who your friends are with whom you love to talk and share your kindness with. Air people need to have connections. Consciously cultivate your friendships. This is a high value of yours.

Ask yourself,
"How are my thoughts
imprisoning me?"

$$ax^2 + bx + c = 0$$

$$x^2 + \frac{b}{a}x + \frac{c}{a} = 0$$

$$x^2 + \frac{b}{a}x + \left(\frac{b^2}{4a^2}\right) - \frac{b^2}{4a^2} + \frac{c}{a} = 0$$

$$\frac{b^2}{4a^2} \qquad \frac{c}{a}$$

$$\pm \sqrt{\frac{b^2}{4a^2}} -$$

$$\pm \sqrt{\frac{b^2 - 4ac}{4a^2}}$$

$$\frac{b}{2a} \pm \sqrt{\frac{b^2 - 4ac}{4a^2}}$$

$$\frac{-b \pm \sqrt{b^2 - 4ac}}{2a}$$

Chapter 10

AIR WOMEN

If you want to know the details, if you want to hear a good story, or find out about a good book to read, ask an Air woman. My friends and family all say that I'm in the "know," and it's true, I can talk about almost anything. I am curious about life, especially people. I would love to be Casper the Friendly Ghost, so I could peek into people's houses, and see how they live, what they do in their day. I am hopelessly curious, maybe even nosey.

I am aware of how people look; I notice their clothes and the way they talk and act. I am conscious of colors and styles. I too like to be well dressed. I have my own style. I am attracted to the off beat personality, as well as the classical "pretty" people." I notice who is wearing the latest styles, for good or bad. But I always return to my own tastes; I am a trendsetter and an individual.

I am into design of all sorts, from the label on the shampoo bottle, to the decor in your house, to the cut of your dress. Colors speak to me. I am one to notice details and then later to talk or write about what I have seen. I am a good reporter and writer.

Social

I can sit at an airport and just watch the people go by. Friends open their hearts easily to me because they know that I am genuinely interested in what they have to say. People often confide in me. I know which questions to ask. I will inquire about your job, your family, your health and happiness. I never forget a face. Your name, now that's another story. At times, my interest in people and their stories can be compulsive and even a bit invasive. Just tell me when it is none of my business – I'll back off.

Reading is one of my pastimes. I read magazines of all kinds and books on just about any subject. Biographies, history, and stories about rich and famous people are my favorite. If I could just find the time to study astrology, or numerology, or a language. I have a bit of knowledge on many topics – I am someone who can skim a book and "get it.'

One of my dreams is to return to school or to take a course on something unfamiliar, even spiritual; it's just that time shrinks around me; I am always busy. My social calendar is full; my family life is so busy.

I have been called the camp counselor, the mediator, the therapist. I want everyone to have a turn at sharing his or her hearts. Harmony at all costs is the theme of my life. I cannot stomach it when people fight or are tense. I am the mediator to help everyone feel good about themselves. Sometimes this creates difficulties, as I am not a very good judge of character; I am learning about discernment. I am learning that not everyone is what they appear.

Relationships

Relationships are a constant fascination for me; they are the "never ending" stories that capture my interest. My girl friends are very important to me. I feel validated through talking; some men find all my words too much. I always have my female friendships to get support from. If I am left for too long on my own with no one to talk to, my mind spins and can drive me crazy. I feel soothed when I can get my thoughts out. It is difficult for me to keep a secret. I have a special pouch for my cell phone that fits neatly into my purse. I am known to use the telephone freely.

Talking is how I nourish and support my relationships. When I was young, I trusted people too much and was hurt. Now I tend to hold back until I am sure of you. You can count on me to be loyal once we have established that we really are friends.

In the beginning, when I first meet a man, he often gets the wrong idea about me. It appears that I am a socialite, easy and outgoing. The truth is, my heart is the last to open. It takes me time to really trust. I maintain my independence because when I get hurt I am not comfortable emotionally and I feel inadequate.

If communication is essential in my friendships, this goes double for the lover I am with. If my partner cannot intellectually match me, I become bored or frustrated. It is not easy for me to talk about emotions with men. I want to share, but if he does not listen well, I will get cold. It is important to be able to talk about the ordinary day-to-day events as well as the emotional stuff. Tell me what you think; to be intellectually stimulated is a big turn-on for me.

I have learned that men have less need to talk, so I nurture my women friendships in a very deliberate way. I tell them what I can't say to my guy, and I have my journal, which has proved a great help to me. I read in a self-help book (I love books on psychology) that journaling can be a healthy tool, and it works for me.

Family

Too much quiet time or empty space feels cold and dreary to me. I need to hear the sound of loved ones' voices and feel the warmth of their presence. Parties or gatherings for any reason appeal to me and I am happy to arrange family events or social holidays. It is a pleasure to schedule and organize, just don't ask me to do the cooking – and remember, I can take on too much and can become irritable. I am often late, and then friends get upset. But when I do arrive, I will do my best to make everyone happy.

Children and I often connect instantly; they seem to recognize the child in me, and we talk. They allow me into their child's world because they trust me. I treat them as equals. Young people have always enchanted me, although I can get impatient if they are stubborn or unreasonable. I am an active mom, though I still find ways to maintain my own life and can feel guilty about my style; sometimes I think I should be Donna Reed. Rarely am I what I think I "should" be.

I can get in trouble when I have the urge to meddle in my family's personal lives. I have learned to stop asking them too many questions. I try not to talk endlessly; I know that I can irritate people. It is just not easy for me to stop when I need to talk. There are times when my temper flares and I may say things that I later regret. When I am organized and everything is running smoothly, I can be gentle and easy-going.

Please forgive me if I talk too much, or ask you too many questions and forget to wait for your answers. I will apologize easily and forgive just as easily. Accept my energized personality. I am alive, bright, and full of good ideas. Just remember the song, "Girls Just Want to Have Fun" – that's me they were singing about.

Work

At work, I can handle several assignments, clients, or projects at the same time. At home, I do the same; I can converse with a friend, watch television, cook a meal, and fold the laundry all without losing my focus. I am an energetic and committed worker, although I occasionally take on more work than I can handle.

Repetitive projects bore me and my mind can wander if I lack stimulation. Sometimes I miss appointments or I am late; promptness and reliability are not my strong points. I know that I need to do less and pace myself, but it is not easy for me. My co-workers and friends say that my charm allows me to get away with my sloppiness.

I collect inventive systems or gadgets that can make living fast and easy. The Internet has become my favorite communication playground; it is a great way to stay in touch and it is so much fun – all the shopping, not to mention all the information I can gather. I love to take short trips through the Internet to other worlds.

Analyzing the advantages and disadvantages of any situation comes easily to me. People tell me I am smart. I can be very knowledgeable on many subjects, but, for some reason, I don't have much confidence in my knowledge. I know that I am a dilettante; I know a lot about a little, but depth is not my specialty.

I can be indecisive and need to ask the advice of the experts. Often it turns out that I did know enough to make an informed decision. There is one advantage in being unsure of myself: I have learned how to ask the right questions and determine the accuracy of the answers.

Chapter 11

AIR MEN

Communication is my specialty. I am a thinker with a powerful desire to know and understand. My wide interests can include complex scientific theories, esoteric arts, or practical business pursuits. I am intensely curious. I love to read. I can be an efficient and tireless researcher. I am good at gathering data, asking questions, and observing.

One of my obvious talents is the ability to make people laugh. I have a great sense of the absurd. Even in life's sadness I am able to raise spirits with my humor. Unfortunately, I may at times use this gift to my own detriment by deflecting emotions that I am afraid to feel, or by drowning issues in a flood of words. Emotionally, I can be insensitive. The cool life of the intellect is where I am comfortable. I can talk about emotions, analyze, or witness them in others, but actually to feel them personally is painful for me.

I am a pragmatic and logical person. I am willing to consider just about any point of view, especially if the person presenting it has done research and it is substantial. Religion as an academic subject could be appealing to me, but the zealot's path would not lure me from my analytical course. For me to believe in the existence of a soul without factual support would be a lengthy, intellectual stretch. I thrive on facts, although I often entertain whimsical thoughts just for the fun of it.

I cannot tolerate intellectual stagnation; I am always reading or studying with a highlighter in hand. The theory that nature abhors a vacuum could apply to me as well. I am always filling in when I sense there is something missing. Impatience and boredom can plague me. I have a low tolerance for boring details or endless repetition.

It is easy for me to maintain a positive attitude about life. I do not understand brooding, negative people. My attitude is, "Pick yourself up – change your life." There are no limits in life if you believe in yourself.

Social

I am an extroverted personality. I love to socialize. I do not like to be alone for long. I am up for any opportunity to hold court and discuss my latest discovery. If I am not permitted to express myself, I will go elsewhere for the stimulation and the audience that I crave.

Relating to people who are slow, quiet, and non-communicative is tedious for me; I have always thought that it is enlightening to talk about our experiences. My attitude is, "When in doubt talk, turn on the television or radio, something to keep me occupied. If my mind is active, it will not slide into negativity."

I can organize and coordinate anything. I am the ultimate networker; I make friends wherever I go. Telephones are my specialty; unfortunately, I often misplace my telephone book or forget where I am supposed to be. I have to write everything down. It has been said that my charm compensates for my absent-minded personality.

During a conversation, if I already know what someone is trying to say, I will interrupt or fill in their sentences. If what is being said is obvious and I have to listen to simplistic explanations, I will lose my concentration and detach. I am the exception to any rule. If everyone does something in a familiar way, following the same path repeatedly, I tend to redesign and create a different approach.

Relationships

With women I can easily become the attentive romantic and just as quickly turn indifferent. I am often indecisive in love until a solid connection is established. Friendship and a strong mind are what attract me first. Because I love to flirt, my partner may not have total confidence in my loyalty or honesty. As I mature, I notice the need to flirt subsides. When I find a partner who really does capture my attention, I am loyal and can focus in on relationship. It is important that I am able to express my fantasies openly within the relationship; after I speak to them I do not feel the need to manifest my fantasies. I long for honesty and to be understood.

When people slow me down because they do not understand me, I will either give way and surrender (I hate to be irrational, I hate to fight), or I will detach. It is easier for me to rationalize and live in my head than to feel the anger or sadness. I can shut things out and just not think of my fantasies. Once in a while my emotions do surface. When this happens, the discomfort forces me to reestablish my detachment. I feel most comfortable when life is easy and light.

Frequently, I need a change of direction. Intellectually, I embrace change as natural and necessary. However, what is not so obvious is that emotional changes make me feel insecure. Only after a lot of talking and thinking can I make the change.

Family

I am sure the Pied Piper was an Air man. Children love me and I love them. I am a great parent because I am interested in staying in tune with what is current; how teenagers think, and what they are doing in school. I am good at letting kids be themselves and talking to them on their level. When the kids get tangled up in emotions or frustration, I tend to back off and let their mom handle that; I am not good when tempers fly and tears drop. I would rather be the fun dad, not the reprimanding or disciplinarian one.

Work

I have a good memory for trivia; I am analytical and a strong critic. When I am interested, reading instructions and figuring out the details is easy for me, otherwise my impatience will force me to use the hit-and-miss approach, and then I can be hazardous to people or objects and especially to machinery. I am interested in computers for they allow me to communicate and access information from unlimited sources. When I get frustrated with them, I know how to seek the expert's advice. I know what I am good at and what I am not good at.

I can make money playing the stock market, in creative design or inventing unique products. I continually think of things that are out of the ordinary. I could be a lawyer, a computer whiz, a professor of linguistics, a creative inventor, or a writer. I am interested in teaching and support groups that sponsor education and humanitarian efforts.

I do not understand the path of followers. I am, however, open-minded enough to allow others to do as they want. I am passionate about the rights of the individual. I will stand up when the underdog is treated unfairly, and I will fiercely defend the rights of the accused.

I am a good spokesperson. If I am not allowed to be my own creative leader, I get bored and refuse to follow. I can become rebellious and irreverent if I do not receive the attention that I deserve.

When my words come from my heart and not my head, there is a chance that I will know love and consistency and therefore be trustworthy. My greatest challenge is to speak from my heart, to find my deep feelings and express them. Can you help me? I am a good student if someone would just explain to me the value of emotions. I long to be understood, eccentric as I may appear. Will you listen to me and help me understand my heart?

Chapter 12

THE STORY OF EARTH

"When all the trees have been cut down,
when all the animals have been hunted,
when all the waters are polluted,
when all the air is unsafe to breathe,
only then will you discover you cannot eat money."

—CREE PROPHECY

Meet Dave and Ann, two people from very different backgrounds who run a family-owned lumber business with some hundred employees, many of whom have been working with the company for over thirty years. They made a conscious decision not to have children. Their family is the community they work with and the people they care about.

When their employees are in need, Dave and Ann have helped them pay off their debts – $45,000 to one man alone. They pay the debts off – a gift, not a loan. They've put employees through school, paying one hundred percent of the tuition. They've given employees money for down payments on homes, and they've provided dirt-cheap rent in forty residences – paid for in cash; no high-interest loans for Earth-born folk.

I was speechless when they said, "We could do so much more." They simply love to give.

Though Ann and Dave are from entirely different backgrounds, their lives together work as a classical yin/yang symphony.

Dave grew up in a morally solid and financially stable household with hard-working parents. He inherited the business from them. He is very masculine, independent, and self-motivated. A double Taurus, he embodies the best of Earth values: the joy of working, serving out of a pure desire to give, and strong perseverance to never quit – even when the arduous task ahead is tedious, repetitive, and predictable. Work is his pleasure: he gives each action all he's got.

> Earth values the joy of working, serving out of a pure desire to give, and strong perseverance never to quit – even when the task ahead is tedious, repetitive, and predictable.

Ann came from the opposite side of the street: alcoholic parents, drug-addicted brothers, and more childhood trauma than a season of contrived TV dramas. She is a hound dog that sniffs out the pain of others; always looking out for them and exceptionally loving. Ann's wisdom is born out of her deep hardship. She doesn't complain or play into the victim role. Her work ethic and her ability to care for those less fortunate is why she is in this chapter. She is emotionally wise and has done the serious study required to have learned how to soothe and heal her wounds. Her life has taught me about how switching on the Observer results in compassion.

Despite their differences, as fate would have it, these two were destined to be together and accomplish great work. She got a job with his company and over time, as they worked together, their relationship grew.

As is often true of Earth people, Dave has a great respect for his many mentors, one of whom was his father. He was taught how to work. And because of Dave's personality type and his phenomenal work ethic, the business naturally prospered and flourished. Tall, lanky, hands-on, Dave always stayed well after hours putting away inventory or taking care of all the things that needed tending, never shying away from the laborious physical work necessary to move lumber.

He grew strong, and wise, by putting in the effort. Over a ten-year period, he and Ann and their team transformed the family business from annual sales of $100,000 and ten employees into a company with over one hundred employees and annual sales in the tens of millions.

When you listen to Dave, you're not surprised that he expanded the family business: "I love making lists. Some people say, 'Tomorrow's another day,' but not me. Today is a good day to get something done. The opportunities I've had in my life have been because I've taken advantage of things, worked hard, and gone the extra mile. I get things done. It's hard for me to be around people who don't want to better themselves. In some ways, we get what we deserve in life. You make choices, and those choices create your life."

Sounds tough, doesn't it? You probably think that Dave drives his employees hard, expects them to sacrifice for the company, and happily fires "lazy" employees. "He's an Amazon," Ann says of her partner when he is not in the room, "He looks tough, but he's a marshmallow inside."

Dave is concerned with the well-being of the local animals and the land. He and Ann bought dozens of acres of land in their neighborhood to protect against development and convert the acreage to public use. He had to fight Native American groups, the federal government, the state government, and even some of his neighbors to do it.

"How did you fight all those people at once?" I asked.

"Oh," Dave said with a laugh, "I don't fight. People throw up roadblocks, sure. But I know they can't stand at the roadblock forever. So in the meantime I just pour myself into other projects and check back now and again. They get tired of manning their roadblocks. Then I go after what I want, and I get it. I got all that land turned into public-use land, so it can always be enjoyed by our community, forever."

Because of Dave and Ann there is now a wildlife refuge in their community. The salmon in that area will survive, and the kids at the schools come and learn about the outdoors first-hand. This story excites Ann; she is squealing with delight as she talks. "We get the local schools involved, and have our employees maintain the property. It is so much fun."

It is not unusual for Earth people to have tenacity like this and to enjoy the feeling of accomplishment. But Dave and Ann are unusual because they reach out to others so far past the call of duty; it's almost strange how much they trust the law of giving. Here is another vivid example…

> Because of Dave and Ann, there is now a wildlife refuge in their community. The salmon in that area will survive, and the kids at the schools will come and learn about the outdoors first-hand.

A year ago, Dave and Ann found out through a neighbor that a couple – the only bi-racial couple in their neighborhood – had suffered badly in the recession. They were two years behind in their sky-high mortgage payments. The $1.6 million dollar home that they had lived in for twenty years was about to be taken from them. Within a few days their beloved house was going to be sold to the highest bidder. The couple and their six children, and their clan of relatives, would be out on the street with nothing but the clothes on their backs. The financial pressure was crushing their spirits.

Concerned and curious, Ann and Dave walked over to the home to assess the situation. The wife, who was alone, answered the door with caution. She shared her tragic story with them. "Hey, I have a perfect solution! Dave and I can buy the house," Ann jubilantly explained, "and then you can rent it from us!"

In a now-I've-heard-everything tone, the woman suspiciously snarled, "Yeah, right." With eyebrows and doubts raised, she suspected Dave and Ann were part of a scam. "And, pray tell, what do you want in return?"

Not missing a beat, Ann matter-of-factly replied that on their walk over she noticed an antique popcorn maker in the garage. (Dave loves popcorn.) "If we buy your house and you become our renters, I'd like that popcorn maker." The exhausted soon-to-no-longer-be-a-homeowner said nothing. Ann nodded, gave a happy wave good-bye, and she and Dave strolled home hand in hand.

The next day Dave and Ann attended their first-ever auction to learn the rules of the foreclosure game. Earth people move slower than most, always respectful of protocol: they usually research whatever they are going to buy. However, this time they had no time. Ann figured out how to connect with the auctioneer in charge, jumped in and bought the house. Innocent and sincere, with their many cashier checks in hand (during such an auction you must have the cash on hand), they scored! Right place, right time. On the spot, Dave and Ann owned the house for $860,000.

Immediately after signing the contracts Ann called the women and said: "I hope this isn't an inconvenient time. I'm coming by to get that popcorn maker. We bought your house."

When they arrived with deed in hand, the awe-struck homeowners welcomed them in with a tsunami of grateful tears. They spread their good news and within hours they had ordered everybody to unpack their stuff. Months and years of worry crumbled in a moment. Miracle of miracles – they were staying home!

Dave and Ann gave them three months rent-free to help them get back on their feet. They fixed the roof, installed a new water heater, and paid an outstanding electric bill. Ann and Dave charged the new renters only about one-quarter of the local market price for rentals. "We'll give 'em a year," Ann says. "Then we'll happily sell them back their house."

"For the full market price?" I queried.

Ann says, "Nah. We just want to get our money back. They're a great couple."

In the past 75 years, most of us have lost our relationship with tribal living: to take care of the other. Modern-day theory says: You are all you have. Take care of your family and self above all else. And, by the way, be sure to keep your eye on the guy behind you because he, too, is self-serving and has no interest in your well-being or your family's.

Evolved Earth people teach by example. Dave and Ann embody the I'll-cover-your-back-and-you'll-cover-mine philosophy.

> Evolved
> Earth people
> teach by example.

You might be thinking now, "Jeez, don't Earth people have any variations?" No, they don't. Earth people live by traditions. Rituals make them feel safe and secure. They are predictable and stable. Loyalty is their middle name. They are true-blue, and they go beyond the call of duty to ensure completion (and perfection).

> *"Once I was in Victoria, and I saw a very large house. They told me it was a bank and that the white men place their money there to be taken care of, and that by and by they got it back with interest. We have no such bank; but when we have plenty of money or blankets, we give them away to other chiefs and people, and by and by they return them with interest, and our hearts feel good. Our way of giving is our bank."*

—Chief Maquinna, Nootka

Earth people are even practical about their love. "Every year on our anniversary, we review our relationship – what worked, and how we can grow better. We're both extremely driven, and we keep each other on our toes," said Ann.

It's not all work and no play. Each year, Ann and Dave give away $10,000 in cash prizes at the company's Easter egg hunt. Last year's Fourth of July fireworks show for their workers cost them $20,000 and spare change.

They provide Christmas gifts for 100-300 employees at the winter gala. In between holidays, they organize food drives, collect clothing for the needy, and donate to all kinds of animal shelters and senior citizen charities. Wow.

They are never-ending givers.

"How can you afford to do all of this?" I ask. "I mean, the expense must be huge!

"It's simply doing the right thing," Dave responded. "Because there are so many families split up and scattered all over nowadays, we're creating community – a place where people can raise families, provide their kids good schools, and help one another get ahead in life. It's all about people."

What goes around, comes around. It's a truth that Dave is so lucky that even the casino's slot machines give to him – he is always the biggest winner: perhaps he is lucky, although I wouldn't call it "luck." Dave gives and works and creates all day, every day – and life happily recycles his magic right back to him. This is an Earth law; that what goes out comes back.

Oh, and one last thing… Dave and Ann do everything anonymously: these aren't their real names. They don't want their philanthropy exposed or to be common knowledge. "If it's known what we do," Dave says, "people will give us the credit when things go right for them. We want them to take the credit. We want them to feel empowered, rooted, and to do right by their families. At the end of the day, it's about building community, and people coming together."

Chapter 13

WORKING WITH THE ELEMENT OF EARTH

Earth – the four-step element program

In a word, this element is all about practicality, that part of each of us whose feet are planted firmly on the ground. The Earth element explains why you are dependable, grounded, and steady. It is why you are so organized, list details, and get things done. Earth flows through cycles; projects have a beginning, middle, and an end. If you have abundant Earth, you are the one who moves slowly and methodically through each step, promising to stay with the job until it's done. You see, following the directions, living within the guidebook, and striving to do things right is Earth's mandate. You often get labeled as a perfectionist – what you really are is an artist of details.

Earth is the element that compels you to provide, give, and serve. Our planet should be called *Water* because it is blue and made up of water, but it is called Earth. Our mission on Earth is to contribute, manifest, and provide equally for all creatures. These qualities possess vast reserves of loyalty and responsibility. But if your Earth becomes overwhelmed, as Alice Bailey says, *"Glamour and greed are the two most distracting influences in the human psyche, preventing us from remembering our true nature."*

THE STEPS

1. **EXPLORE: Go inside and identify the element's energies and patterns in your life.**

2. **ARTICULATE: Put words to your elemental patterns – speak with a trusted witness, laugh about it together.**

3. **INVESTIGATE: Acknowledge the strengths and shadow-sides. Identify and get familiar with your elemental lessons.**

4. **TRANSFORM: Begin a practice to create a new paradigm.**

The essence of Earth is true-blue, and goes beyond the call of duty. They are workaholics and love to be busy. Just like Mother Earth who is always fertile, Earth's generous nature is constantly giving. Acknowledging the invisible realms can be a stretch for Earth people. Buddha was an Earth sign, and his gift to us was all about non-attachment – probably the most important of Earth's lessons.

Serious and ambitious, Earth people are best suited for work that requires a strong degree of concentration and focus. When Earth people are determined and motivated, they achieve their goals by faithfully plugging away. You also know everything has its proper place. Perhaps you have pulled out your personal label maker, helping others in your world who may not have your keen sense of organization. A value you carry is that *with hard work and following rules you will be successful.* Check your drawers and closets, if you wonder if I am describing you. Do you wear the same clothes way longer than they seem worthy? Perhaps your favorite way to spend the day is cleaning out your drawers or working on the garage. It is the good feeling you get when the job is done. Crossing things off your list is like sex for you.

> Do you have an unspoken dress code you follow, with everything in order in your closet by color and season?

Earth is about the material world and the almighty buck. Earth is the part of you that's down-to-earth, that wants results, wants to know how long it is going to take, and how much money it is going to cost and make. Balancing the checkbook is your pastime. A natural role for you is being the accountant or banker for family and friends, helping everybody prosper.

Too much Earth – you run the risk of being preoccupied and overly attached, self-critical with unreasonably high standards, and you never seem to get it right.

Too little Earth – you find yourself with no practicality or focus on getting things done, financially suffering from lack of budgets and a messy world.

You know you have good Earth when you are practical and instinctively flow with the natural cycles of the earth; when you do the mundane activities of day-to-day life, cooking, cleaning, and whistling as you work, and while being kind to others without judging them for not being like you.

Here are the big questions when you *EXPLORE* Earth:

- How do we accept the ebbs and flows and allow change to be easy?
- How do we serve others while serving ourselves?
- How do we become less attached to results and enjoy life's journey?

Take time to go inside, reflect, and identify the habitual patterns of your Earth personality, the places where your attachment to security and the practical world has captured you. When you are overly focused on finances, you scare yourself. Notice your internal dialogue that is self-critical and has convinced you that you have not done your best or done enough. If you feel stuck, try asking yourself, "Do I have faith in this world?" Do you feel exhausted, because you are always the one doing what needs to be done? Create a list of what you have to do. The "have to do's" are often the places you are overworking. Let yourself become conscious of the part of you who has placed the bar of success beyond your reach. You are doing far more than you realize – ask someone for feedback and you will realize I am telling you the truth.

Review the elemental survey (earth) you completed earlier on: are you in touch with the practical and grounded world? Whether your score is low or high, spend a few moments reflecting on ways you have been loyal, practical, and focused. Earth people forget to give themselves appreciation for what they do.

Once you identify how in touch you are with the practical world, begin to use the wisdom of the Observer to see your patterns at a distance. List all your accomplishments, then ask yourself "What am I good at?" Explore your strengths.

Often when your Earth element is out of sync, fear creeps in, leaving you feeling insecure and like you don't have enough, allowing your inner critic to start the self-judgments. This inner critic can easily grab hold of you, pushing you to do more, which often becomes the "I should" list. The Shoulds are good at keeping you busy, doing and performing, chasing a finish line that keeps moving out of your reach. Whew, time to get off the treadmill for a bit.

Remember to turn off your ego – your internal critic and judge – and turn on the Observer, your voice of compassion, and witness your human self and strengths.

> The "Shoulds" are good at keeping you busy doing and performing, chasing a finish line that keeps moving out of your reach.

Earth Energies and Key Words

- Consistent, stable, solid, and predictable
- Loves to eat – "Foodies," into organic, vegan; checks labels, ingredients, additives
- Grounded and down-to-earth
- Loves to spend and make money
- Enjoys sensuality, loves the human body just as it is
- Obsessed with plants, herbs, natural medicine
- Planners and builders who get pleasure from structure
- Loyal and trustworthy
- Works hard and forgets to have fun
- Likes doing the steps to get things done – enjoys how-to books
- Likes routine, repetition, consistency
- Functional, practical, purposeful things are valued
- Quality-minded and wants perfection
- Clean, organized and uncluttered
- Slow and simple – might be seen as boring
- Financially savvy
- Substantial – designer labels, into high quality
- Hard to move; stubborn; highly opinionated, controlling
- Result-oriented; timelines, records, and schedules
- Research-oriented and results-oriented
- Kinesthetic and sensual – likes being in the body
- Always thinking of what needs to happen next
- Gets everything done and has no problem maintaining things
- Focused on sustainability, environmental well-being
- Critical, judges self, holds back feelings
- Generous and service-oriented

Strengths of Earth

- Hard-working and focused, working to achieve results – have the ability to complete what needs to be done
- Ruled by ambition, loyalty and integrity; a devoted employee, friend and companion
- Appreciates creature comforts and enjoys nurturing others
- Contributes, manifests and provides equally for all creatures
- Plans and builds carefully for the future
- Accepts hardship as a reality of life. Self-reliant and resilient

Shadow of Earth

- Exaggerated need for material possessions and physical resources
- Don't believe they are doing a good enough job. All work, and no play
- Expressing emotions is difficult; keeps busy to avoid them
- Obsessive follower of rules; minimal flexibility with game plans
- Clings to cautious, conservative action; wants an insurance plan and everything clean-cut and clear
- Defensive; strict, and demanding. Smothers loved ones by possessiveness
- Unwilling to make changes once settled into a routine
- Arrogant leaning towards "know-it-all"
- Appear organized, smart and confident but inside their head they believe the opposite
- Stingy, doesn't share, hoards things and money

Now *ARTICULATE* and voice whatever your Earth traits are. Read them out loud. This is easy for you guys, as you love lists. Find a trusted companion to share your list with. If you're open to feedback, ask them to edit your list and remove anything that describes the pattern as a "should" – and exchange it for "I want to." If you don't really want to do what the Should says, then take a guilt-free card and remove it. So much of what motivates you is obligation or over-responsibility.

EARTH people will relate to the following:

- Others consider me to be practical and grounded
- I clean or organize when I am upset
- I am thorough and deliberate when I work
- I love good food and am sensitive to tastes and smells
- Budgeting and saving money is important to me
- I prefer to be in control and to find myself in charge
- Being in nature is essential for me
- I am goal-oriented and I get results
- People can rely on me and consider me dependable
- I am slow to change

Practice saying the mantra, "Nowhere to go and nothing to do"; this is the art of relaxing. To enjoy Earth, walk in nature and relish a good meal. Think bite-size and one foot in front of the other – walk slowly as you cultivate this element and begin to enjoy the natural cycles of the earth. Earth hates to change, so this may not be easy.

To *INVESTIGATE* your elemental lessons, take the attitude of an apprentice who is gathering data and learning a new skill. Ask questions, and explore your habits and patterns.

Beware of your need to be in control and in charge to keep everything in order and on schedule. Learn to use the Observer to laugh at your need to be in control and in charge. Receiving is not your strength. It is okay for you to depend on others and let them do it their way. We learn more about giving when we can also receive. "Really?" you are thinking, "Easier said than done."

The key for Earth is to relax and to realize this simple truth: all that is needed will be provided. Even when you are in winter cycle and your manifestation is slowing down, you can trust. The inner world is equally important. Peace and trust is much more important than reaching all the high goals you have set. Healthy Earth knows the importance of

> The key for Earth to relax is to realize this simple truth: that all that is needed will be provided.

rolling with the punches when things don't happen according to the best-laid plans. When Earth is healthy and at a relaxed pace, you will know how to be spontaneous and play – with less attention on telling everyone what they need to do.

Earth people are patient and precise teachers. Being a student is far more difficult. Be a student of simplicity. When you begin to find fulfillment from simple pleasures, without using the outer world as a measuring stick, there is a calm that settles in. One gentle way to release your old patterns is to give yourself new permissions.

Permissions for Earth

- I will learn ways to be comfortable to take risks and let go of worrying.
- I will remember to relax and enjoy, and release inner dialogue focused on what's not being done.
- It is okay for me to lower my standards. Often they are unreasonably high and I do not even know it.
- I can bask in my accomplishments and recognize all that I do.
- I can accept and love the parts of me that value purpose and function, and see them as fun.
- I can acknowledge simple, hard truths. I can accept my fate and know that every problem is not necessarily meant to be solved or fixed.
- It is ok to slow down and be methodical – the turtle won the race.
- Just like Buddha, I will let go of attachment to results and things (good luck!).

Now it is time to *TRANSFORM* and change the old story. You might:

- Seek the advice of others. Learn ways to let yourself change and grow through the trials, errors, and victories of others.
- For a change, do nothing. And do it fully without fear. See how in doing nothing, you can relax and enjoy the moment.
- Try acting on impulse every now and then. Even though there is a sense of security in repetition, understand that things do not remain the same forever.

- Practice saying these sentences: "I need your help." "I like the way you do that." "Will you teach me?" "I was wrong."

- Ask others, whom you consider having personal tastes and philosophies different from yours, to explain them. Listen with genuine curiosity and notice the places where you are aligned – and gently nudge your awareness towards acceptance of what you don't understand and know.

- Begin to find ways to let go of your of attachments. We come into this world empty-handed, and we ought to live with our heart as the measuring stick of our success.

The right use of Earth is honoring and giving gratitude for Mother Earth by always thanking her for Nature's bounty. Take a walk, smell the flowers, notice the sunset. Never be too busy to notice Mom's beauty. The dance of the Earth's soul is to give selflessly. Once an Earth person begins to cultivate the wisdom to be less attached to results and just enjoy the journey, they relax and they begin to slow down and trust the process.

If you wish to bring the element of Earth into balance or to create a practice to maintain stable healthy Earth, here are some suggestions to get you started.

Meditation

Learning meditation is the short answer to the question of how to cultivate humility. Using your breath, feel your sitting bones on the ground. Imagine a long cord starting at your tailbone dropping down into the earth. Now see a bright beam reaching from the top of your head up to the stars. With each inhalation, breathe your energy from down the cord connecting you to Mother Earth, up through the top of your head.

Dabble Regularly in the Land of the Practical

Prepare a meal at least twice a week, promise yourself you will clean a closet or balance your bank account, water your plants, tend to your garden. The practical world is a spiritual avenue when approached with reverence. Indeed, even the most mundane act has sacredness to it.

Give Back

The right use of Earth is sharing and philanthropy, and consideration of the generations to come. Enjoy being generous and sharing. Be philanthropic and give to charities, or volunteer. Be honest with yourself and ask: "How do I give back to the Earth in my day-to-day living, work, and service?" Find a way to embrace an attitude of reverence and gratitude, and share with those in your life or in your community your time, talent, and money.

Honor and Create Rituals

Earth types confuse their love of "same old, same old" with the mundane – when actually they are rituals. When you drink a cup of coffee or have a glass of wine, notice that this can be a sacred act. Even washing the dishes after a dinner party can go from being a step on your "to-do" list to the pleasure of a ritual; wash each plate while giving thanks for the food, the good conversation, and the time you spent nourishing your body. This is called *mindfulness*.

Renew and Revive with Nature's Gifts

Eat with total pleasure, savor the kiss, and enjoy the sensuality of a stroll outside in nature. Slow down. Find time to dig in the dirt or watch the clouds float by. Appreciate beauty and the sensory experience that a massage, a room filled with incense, or the pleasures of touch provide. Remember to ask yourself regularly, "What do I do to find pleasure?" – a foreign question for an Earth person. Being immersed in earthly tasks is a great way to jump off the track and miss the beauty of the moment. You deserve to relish this life.

Enjoy Life's Little Messes

It is okay to leave a mess, make fun of yourself, laugh at your own idiosyncrasies and know that the outer world is not as important as you think. It is important to let go of the attachment of having everything in order, which is sometimes easier said than done. See if you can leave the dishes undone for just one night or not apologize if you haven't finished everything before your guests arrive. If you are lacking in the element of Earth, turn this one around. See if you can organize a drawer and keep it that way for more than a week. Either way, take a step back and smile at the messes – and try a new way of tackling them with joy.

Chapter 14

EARTH WOMEN

I am practicality incarnate. I know how to make things happen by following through and getting things done just as they should be. I wish that others were like me – and honestly, if you'd let me help you, I could tell you what you'd need to learn. It may appear that I am being judgmental, but I'm not. I believe that if people were willing to listen to me tell them how to be more practical, the world would run more smoothly, and there would be fewer problems. I could definitely teach people how to get things done.

That said, as I've matured I have noticed that not everyone can be practical and follow through like I do. I am trying to accept people just the way they are. This is a learned skill and honestly, it isn't easy for me.

I don't waste time, food, or money. People who throw things away that could be refurbished, or people who don't pass on timeless antiques bother me. I love wood and ancient things. I love history and old photographs. I save things for old time's sake because I value the effort that goes into anything that is made with someone's hands. In an unemotional way I am sentimental.

Social

I was old when I was young and hopefully am getting younger as I am getting older. I am not interested in fun for its own sake, unless there are some redeeming qualities involved – like a humanitarian pursuit, or a charitable cause. Otherwise, I have fun exercising, saving money, and buying things for those that I love. It is fun when you can be functional and entertained at the same time.

I like things concrete and real. I look at labels. I always go for the most expensive dress or jewelry; none of the fake stuff for me, though I will buy from catalogues to save time. I appreciate designers and their quality goods. I am willing to pay the extra dollar to get the real thing. It makes me happy to get exactly what I want at a wholesale price, and I often know the important people in influential places to get the deal.

I love to garden, to cook and eat. I am loyal and reliable. I don't have many friends and am not interested in superficiality. I can follow instructions, read the manual, and take care of the details. I love having animals.

My self-esteem is solid and grounded; I measure my success by my accomplishments. I can get really insecure if I am not feeling strong financially. I don't feel like I am safe without a wad in the bank. I often wonder if people like me because of what I do for them. I am not a thinker as much as a doer. I am not socially warm when it isn't necessary.

Relationships

Relationship to me is a very simple topic. I have certain rules that I follow: be loyal to the one whom you chose and make sure that you give that person your all. When there is a problem, talk it out as soon as possible. Never go to sleep with unfinished business because that will sour your connection later. Never speak of divorce; it is not a choice. Work through issues efficiently and quickly, and keep focused on what really matters.

I am not interested in listening to someone's repetitive problems. Mostly, people don't find me the life of the party. I only have a few close friends and that is fine with me. I wish that there was an instruction manual on how to chitchat and be superficial because I really don't understand all that. I hate small talk.

Sometimes people may think I'm not interesting. Actually, I am a wealth of information on the topics that I know well. Because I excel at what I do, I am very knowledgeable. If you need contacts or solid information, ask me. I like to help people.

Spiritually, I notice that as the years pass I find myself more and more interested in the mystical realm. In my youth, I was a workaholic and had a single eye regarding what was important to me, whether it was relationship, family, or work. As I age, I notice that I find the workaholic thing settling down a bit.

I am good at ritual and repetition. I like to go to church on Sundays and to light candles during a meal and eat healthily. I am good at following a regimen or a schedule. I get mad at myself when I have to slow down.

I *should* myself a lot, like with exercise. I know that it *should* be a regular part of my life. I hate when I don't do it because I gain weight easily and have a slow metabolism. I know where to get the food that I really like and will go to the same market for years and years. I am a loyal buyer; I like predictability and consistency, and I like having relationships that are long-standing and faithful.

Family

Giving to my family is so easy; I clean and cook without even thinking. When I am upset I clean – this is what I do to settle myself down. I am always on time and organized. I wish that others had the same values as I have.

When there are disagreements or emotional upsets, that's just the way it is. I can be offensive and even harsh with my honesty, and yet I don't know how to do it differently. If I don't really care, or can't make a difference, I just won't talk to the person at all and let the problem draw attention to itself in its own sweet time. I know when I am right and it is hard to change my mind.

I am a tough parent, but a good one. I am devoted and attentive to my children. I believe children should learn how to do what they are told. Discipline is very important to me. I treat my kids well and expect the same in return.

At worst it may appear that I am demanding, or at least pushy.

I probably am a bit too patient and therefore I will avoid conflict. Then, when the time comes for change, I resist and even mope around. I am moody but not verbally expressive. It is very, very difficult for me to ask for help.

When I am emotional, there are times when I cannot identify what I am feeling. I tend to deny my feelings and use reason and/or tasks to keep me focused and on target. Emotions are distracting and time-consuming. Surely I will give those I love time to listen to their feelings, it is just hard for me to talk about my own.

I will fight for someone I love, or if my integrity or reputation is in question.

Please be gentle with me. I don't mean to be a know-it-all, or to hurt your feelings.

Work

I am best suited for a leadership position so I can instruct others in how to deal with challenges and difficulty. I have learned from the school of hard knocks. I had a childhood that required I grow up at an early age and be responsible.

I find it very difficult to follow a leader when the person is not as efficient as I am, or if they don't know how to do something. This was true even in my childhood. I was somewhat disrespectful to any man who used his power over me without good reason. As I age, I am easier on authority figures, mostly because, more times than not I have become one.

I excel at work that requires a strong degree of concentration and focus. I am not good at quick change, nor am I interested in someone's airy-fairy ideas. I am a serious and ambitious individual. I will do something for years and be faithful and consistent at it.

Work and my ambition have my undivided attention. Retirement is not easy for me.

Chapter 15

EARTH MEN

Actions speak louder than words. I'm sure this was said by an Earth person because it's true, you can only trust someone by his or her actions. While I often feel strongly about someone when I meet them, I try to suspend judgment until I see their work. The proof is in the pudding. I am always impressed when I hear that someone went to a prestigious school or has strong training by a masterful teacher.

I am judgmental. I have criteria for how things ought to get done. I often carry on the interests that my family had before me. I am a creature of habit. I love history. Coin collections, stamp collections, even rocks and mineral collections belonging to my grandparents are things that I will keep around for a long time.

Antiques and historical remnants need to be cared for. Clearly an Earth person invented the concept of storage. I can save things for years and years just in case I might need them someday. Then again, I can be a minimalist. I can go for a long time and not buy a thing until I know what I need and it fits perfectly.

I believe everyone should learn how to take care of things. Respect is a major issue for me. I demand it. Respect for money and a strong work ethic is the foundation of what I stand upon. This is the value system that I teach others. I am often a teacher. I know that I am not as consistent as I would like to be. I hear myself repeat the line I learned from my Dad, "Don't do what I do, do what I say."

I am an extremist. I have been known to buy three pairs of the same shoes, the same pants and the same shirt if I like them. I can't help myself; I know what I like and will do whatever it takes to get what I want. I have very particular taste buds and cannot compromise or settle for less. I am known to wear the same clothes day in, day out if I am working and don't have time to think about cosmetics.

Social

I am a quiet person. I do not like social occasions unless there is a professional reason that I am there. If you get me talking about my favorite interest in business, or art or cars I can't stop talking. Another topic I like is the means and avenues to make money. On these topics I have a lot to say. In fact, I can dominate a conversation on a few topics when I really know my stuff. It's just that I do not like to talk for its own sake and I hate small talk.

Although I try not to be sexist and chauvinistic, I pride myself on allowing women to be heard. The truth, however, is that my nature compels me to take care of women and children – especially my family. I always want to provide and help those who need it. I don't mean to be demeaning, but we men are physically stronger and historically we have been the financially responsible party and the ones who make the big decisions.

Relationships

To me, relationships are just like running a business. There must be agreements, mutual support, and consistency. I am truly loyal and concerned about making everyone happy. To me this means stability, generosity, and helpfulness.

I love to gift those whom I feel deserve it. I am eternally loyal. Once betrayed, there is no going back. I have a memory like an elephant and will not forget if a lack of integrity has been displayed. I can cut off my emotions when I deem it important. I have very high standards for others as well as for myself.

In fact, I criticize others as I do myself. I know what is possible in the name of goodness, and when I am less than "good," I am disappointed. I know what I should be eating, how often I should be exercising and how much I should be saving – it is not easy when I break the pattern and indulge. I love routine and consistency. When I break the pattern, I get stingy and can't give to myself or to others. Here is the extremist again; when I am generous I can't give enough, and when I'm financially insecure I count pennies.

I am very conscious about the charities and the causes that I want to give my money to. I am not a big tipper unless I have been served properly. When I give, I give a lot; otherwise I keep track of waste.

Family

My family will be safe when I am around. I am a provider. My style is to always carry my own weight and to help those whom I love. It is my pleasure to give. I am very generous until I feel that I am being taken advantage of, and then I will still give, but not without conditions. We will talk about the return, make a payment plan, an agreement. Gentlemen's handshake is enough for me, unless you betrayed me once before, then we must have it signed, sealed, and delivered. It is difficult for me to receive. This is something that I must learn about.

I am responsible for taking care of the family car. I am responsible for making sure that my family is well dressed and our social obligations are fulfilled. What is mine is yours, inside the family. I am not generous to people I do not know or care about.

I am an emotionally stable person, not overtly happy or fascinating – I am a meat and potato kind of guy; down to earth and predictable. I like a clean house and to put things back where they belong. I like to build things. I notice the details of a house; the woodwork and the finishing.

Organization pervades all that I do. I like to eat the same kinds of food at a consistent time with everyone sitting properly at the table. Table manners are important to me. History has given us laws to live by and I follow these. I am a strict parent. I suppose I could be softer with the kids. I am busy and time is of the essence for me – can't waste it. I will listen to you if you listen to me.

I honor age. The saying, "Respect your elders," to me – this is a truth. There are many truths that I uphold for the sake of family and what I call "honorable behavior."

I assume that I will sit at the head of the table at my house. I always take the first pick of whatever is being served and I assume the role of the household head. I feel best if I can pick up the bill and am insulted if someone else insists and overrides me, though I would never say that. My friendships are with men who I consider to be like blood relations. I hold onto my friendships for years and years, and though I don't talk a lot, my dearest friends know how I feel by my actions.

I don't share my financial status with anyone, even my wife. I am responsible and will share everything I have with her when the time comes. I am private and quiet about what we are worth and how much we have. I love to buy my wife very nice gifts of jewelry and substantial things – like a home and furniture. This is my greatest pleasure.

Work

I am goal-oriented. I am most happy when I am working. When I can provide and help my family, friends, or colleagues, I feel functional and useful. This is a joy to me. I am loyal and dependable. I have a strong desire to excel at what I do.

The only approach I have to my life is to give all that I have to what I consider important. If I can't do it well I would rather not do it at all. Even as a child I was like this. Surprisingly, I can be lazy. If there is something I must do that has no real meaning for me, I just won't do it. When I can really sink my teeth into something, I become super-ambitious.

I am a traditional kind of leader. Although I appear quiet, I know exactly what should be done in a crisis or a demanding situation. I wait until it is obvious that I must take a stand and then I will offer my help. I am not impulsive.

I am not a show-off. I am reserved and even shy. At times I underestimate my abilities because those with more bravado make all the noise and have the charisma. Me, I just do what is necessary. I don't require a lot of attention or even acclaim. What I count on is loyalty, gentleness, and family values. This is what nourishes me.

Though I am ambitious, I can be happy with a menial job.

Chapter 16

THE STORY OF FIRE

Fire never burns lukewarm: it's either hot…or it's hot! Fire is extreme and shows up as great success or embarrassing, horrible failures – and, in some cases, both. The questions are: What do Fire people do with their life force and the cards that fate has dealt them? Are they the hero or the victim?

I am going to tell you two tales that describe Fire. One is the story of Drew and Myra Goodman, founders of Earthbound Farm. Their slow-burning, sustained fire helped change the history of farming. The company they started is the largest grower of organic produce in North America, and they were also the first people to successfully market packaged salads for retail sale.

The other tale is about Colette Baron-Reid, a spiritual teacher and seer. Her story is about how her Fire began in her childhood, burning fast and furious with a self-destructive influence that almost destroyed her gifts and talents. Yet she remembered her purpose. Colette is an example of how to alchemize fire and pain into gold and wisdom.

Fire children are not easy kids. They show up as either the wild kid who is loud and angry – attention getters who are often in detention, never trying very hard, and waiting until they are old enough to do it on their own. Or they are the high achievers who do great in school and stand out. We endearingly call these kids "pistols": they shoot from the mouth.

> Fire children are not easy kids. They show up as either the wild kid who is loud and angry or as the high achiever who does great in school and stands out.

Let's start with Colette – a very successful best-selling author, educator, intuitive counselor and life strategist, radio-show host, coach, psychic, healer, musician, and wife. She has written several books, created four popular oracle card decks, produced two amazing albums, lectures around the world, and has done readings for tens of thousands of people – from the very famous to the ordinary. She can sense things about people and connect to their stories in a way that has everyone believing in magic: it's specific, detailed, and unquestionably accurate. Her life is filled with love and service. Her story is one of emergence – from the very dark to the very light.

Colette was raised in an upper-class life style in Toronto. Her parents were immigrants destined to be more than survivors. Her mother was Jewish, and a survivor of the Holocaust, her Parisian grandfather was killed in Dachau – although her parents withheld that truth from her. Her dad became a self-made millionaire who came to Canada at the age of forty-eight with 14 cents in his pocket.

Colette was well educated and lived under the strict and constant pressure to perform in her academic life. At a young age she handled the pressure with an eating disorder and alcohol. By the time she was a teenager, she was having blackouts. It didn't stop there. It continued with addiction, promiscuity, and a wildness that is entertaining for kids and nightmarish for their parents.

Fire children often have issues with food and weight. They want more of everything – the extra drink, more cake, a bit more chocolate. They are a party waiting to happen, always desperate for escape. Then they quit...and start again: the perfect prelude for a food disorder. They are extremists. Remember, there is no such thing as lukewarm fire.

The moment alcohol touched her lips she immediately wanted more. When drunk, she relinquished "choice." "I felt dirty," she said, "so I sought out the dirtiest places I could find, hoping to uncover a place where I could feel at home. Some part of me knew it wasn't right, but I was getting real good at covering up that little voice."

Then one night, while her intuitive voices were screaming at her to pay attention, she got into a car with a bunch of guys, knowing something horrible was about to happen. And it did. Colette experienced a total loss of power – through gang-rape.

Like a sped-up, time-lapse silent movie of a baby chick bursting free from its mother's egg, great glowing images scampered through her head – snapshots of her assaulters tumbled across her closed eyelids, one after another. In outright terror she "saw" in detail her rapists' own abuse, suffering, and brokenness – first-hand horrors that led them to choose a life so vile. Colette would have to struggle to blind this psychic cinema... because it was too painful, too disturbing.

Fire people cannot explain their psychic abilities or their urge to be

> Fire people cannot explain their psychic abilities or their urge to be self-destructive. They are extremely perceptive and outspoken – and these two qualities get them in trouble.

self-destructive. They are extremely perceptive and outspoken – and these two qualities get them in trouble.

As a teenager, Colette was driving down life's expressway as fast as she could, fueled by impulsive, out-of-control behavior.

After finishing high school, Colette entered college. "I went to law school, but I majored in sex, drugs, and disappointment. I didn't know how to express myself except in those rare moments when I picked up a guitar and let myself sing. The rest of the time, I experienced frustration and pain by hurting myself."

When I asked Colette whether anybody noticed her state, she delivered a huge belly laugh, one that is so uniquely hers. Most Fire people laugh and talk loud, and Colette is no exception. She bellowed, "Deb, the usual relationships that I attracted handed me the matches, lit them, and pulled up a chair to watch me burn. Yes, I got attention but my soul didn't. I was totally driven by the drama, my addictions, and my wounded ego's needs."

Colette dated drug dealers, served cocktails in a strip club, and continued to lose weight thanks to her love affair with crack cocaine. She fell in love with a man who mirrored her own destructiveness and, eventually at the age of twenty-six, hit rock bottom.

These kinds of destructive relationships are classic for someone attracted to drama, as Fire people often are. The person knows they are being hurt, they know they ought to leave, but the addiction to danger is at work. At worst, they stay in the game until they are burnt to a crisp. And so it was for Colette: she lived in her hell for two years.

Colette did not finish law school. Strung out, remorseful, and exhausted, she checked herself into rehab.

While drying out, Colette's spiky black hair adorned the head of her anorexic, matchstick-thin body. Purple spandex pants covered her legs, and her 5-inch stiletto high-heeled boots rarely left her feet, regardless of mud or snow.

It was on one such muddy afternoon while walking the grounds of the recovery center that her heel stabbed the ground and stuck. Halting her parade-like trance, she freed her foot, pausing to notice her surroundings. Next to her was a tree – majestic in height, weather-beaten, silent, and strong. Awestruck, Colette studied the tree like an artist would, looking at it for a very long time, and realized that something had put it there – a force stronger than she, that was underneath, within, and around everything.

In that very long moment her old world died…and a new one was born. Her unhealthy Fire had burned itself out. A tiny seed of new Fire sparked, fed by a connection to God, to love, to the Oneness of everything. This was Colette's ah-ha moment.

She severed herself from her self-destructive lover, and developed a new, nurturing relationship with herself. She rediscovered her singing voice. During her years in recovery she pursued the world of music, scored a record contract with EMI Music, and made two successful albums.

Her recovery healed her "Me, me, me" theme song. She turned to her purpose and discovered a spiritual model and teaching tools to help many. Now, her incredibly generous nature (another Fire characteristic) serves others in big, joyful ways through her psychic ability and deep psychological wisdom. She has trained hundreds of students to cultivate their wisdom to see and use their intuition. Her teachings come out of her direct experience: Fire people are their own authority. They are graduates from their own personal school of hard knocks. Colette mastered the path of recovery…and thereby became a healer.

> Fire people are their own authority. They are graduates from their own personal school of hard knocks.

Now, let's turn to Drew and Myra Goodman, both Fire signs. Their tale carries a sustained, low-burn consistency for over 30 years. They fearlessly followed fate's lead. Unlike the other element-people, who are much more poised and controlled and can follow the "norm," Fire people rewrite the "norm."

Drew and Myra were circling each other way back in the 1980s, when they attended the same New York City high school and lived less than a block apart. They didn't really know each other until they started dating as college students in California.

Myra, who is a few years younger than Drew, graduated high school early. "Myra's in a hurry all the time," said Drew. She was on the fast track, starting college at 16. She created an independent major called Human Perspectives, a combination of anthropology, philosophy, and religion.

During the second semester of her sophomore year, at just 16, Myra traveled to India on an international studies program. With a car, a driver, and an interpreter, she visited secluded villages to talk with rural women about the benefits of a government-sponsored rural development initiative she was researching. But as her research progressed, she discovered that the villages were controlled by the local government and the upper classes, who in general were denying access to the poorest women who could benefit the most.

Myra spent days painstakingly typing her report on an old manual typewriter, assuming that her insightful research would spark some investigation and resolution. But that's not what happened. Because her conclusion hadn't completely validated the success of the initiative, she received a failing grade to ensure that her report would never be submitted.

Myra was outraged. This fierce, young Fire girl thought she was going to influence the Indian government to ensure that their programs actually made a difference for poor women. For the first time in her life, Myra felt powerless. Her tremendous anger and frustration was a turning point. She could no longer enjoy simply satisfying her intellectual curiosity. She felt compelled to take action. At the sweet age of 18, Myra was a revolutionary, angry at the establishment when no one cared about her point of view or her desire to help.

I love that story! It sets the stage for how idealistic and passionate Fire people are when they have a goal and a cause.

Myra told me, "The injustice in life galvanized me. Fairness is one of the things that matters most to me." This is a true Fire sign quality: Fire people always champion the underdog.

Myra was just 20, and Drew 24, when they moved onto their own little Garden of Eden.

They found a small farm in Carmel Valley they could live on in exchange for rent. They knew absolutely nothing about farming, but fate assigned them to become one of the first companies to prove that organic farming is viable on a large scale. Fire people just jump – and ask questions later. Ready, fire, aim. Neither of them had a clue as to what they were doing.

In Drew's words:

"Starting the farm was like being left on a desert island with nothing and having to figure it out. We got a brief tutorial on caring for the raspberries and starting the tractor from the guy who was moving out, but I forgot a pad of paper and was just hoping I'd remember what he said."

Fire people are "wing-it" artists. They jump in where others would stand aside or walk away as fast as they can.

"When it was time to apply the pesticides," Drew said, "I walked out to the shed where the chemicals were kept. I opened the door and there was this awful poisonous scent. I was scared to be in there. It gave me the heebie jeebies. I thought to myself, 'I don't want to eat this stuff, I don't want touch this stuff. We just won't use it.'"

> Fire people are "wing-it" artists. They jump in where others would stand aside or walk away as fast as they can.

Myra continued, "Growing up in New York City, where you never see a piece of farmland, you don't know about these chemicals. You certainly don't see or taste them on your produce; you don't even know they are there. Toxic chemicals are designed to kill insects and weeds, and I wondered what else will they kill? How can we use them to grow food for human consumption with a clean conscience? There has to be a way to farm without them."

Drew recalls the beginning of Earthbound Farm:

"We put a sign out on our driveway and sold raspberries for a $1.50 a basket. People would come and say, 'They are 99 cents at the grocery store,' and we would say, 'Yes, but ours are organic and taste so much better!' We never let that argument about price stop us."

Drew and Myra worked long hard days, and being too tired to cook, would usually eat quick dinners like frozen pizza. They were growing delicious specialty salad greens right outside their kitchen window, but at the end of the day they were too worn out to harvest them for their own dinner. Eventually they started washing and bagging enough salad for the whole week every Sunday. And when it was as fast and easy as opening a bag, they'd eat healthy greens every night. Pre-washed salad in a bag. What a concept!

When they tried to sell their pre-washed specialty salads beyond their local area, Drew did the cold-calling through the phone book. Not an easy job in that era when salad meant heads of iceberg lettuce. He received rejection after rejection.

According to Drew, "Myra would hear me talking loudly on the phone, pushing our packaged salads onto every potential client. I remember her asking me once, 'How long are you going to call this guy for? He doesn't want our product.' I told her, 'I am going to call him every day until he does.' And I did. I called him every day for about six months. I kept calling and calling, to prove my point I knew that what we had was good for him and everyone concerned, and I wanted him to agree."

Fire people are pushy. They will not take "No" for an answer. They love to help, they love to compete, and they love to prove you wrong. They love a challenge and hard work.

According to Drew, "The truth is, we were constantly told this will never work. Few people were convinced we could make a living selling packaged baby greens or farming organically." Earthbound Farm's annual sales are now over $500 million.

This is a story is of perseverance and determination. Myra and Drew had no plans to be the biggest grower of organic produce– they say they were just following their destiny.

Can you feel the Fire?

What these two stories have in common are fiery characters who have walked past their limitations, past their family's pain, straight to success. Myra's parents were also Holocaust victims. Both women took their difficult lineage and lifted it up. Nothing can stop the powerful fate of a Fire person once they follow their destiny.

Fire can go in two directions. It can inspire an Olympic athlete to greatness or it can burn holes in one's liver and be a source of depression and obesity. The question a Fire person needs to ask is: Who am I serving? Is it my ego and the struggle? Or is it my mission and my gifts? Colette claimed her gifts, rather than taking the self-destruction path, and she has been serving ever since.

What will it take for you to find your mission? To never take "No" for an answer, remember the stories of Drew and Myra, and that of Colette. They instinctually walked right into their huge success – and in the process made a contribution to all of us. They did this without a plan: it was destined and intense as they followed their passion.

Fate will have her way with you if you just say, "Yes." Do you need to fire up your life, start again and get back in the game, through honesty and humility like Colette did? Are you ready to give yourself to a cause, to give freely, to volunteer and pour out your life force like the Goodmans did? The short answer is: Just do something. Go ahead. Let the fire roar.

Chapter 17

WORKING WITH THE ELEMENT OF FIRE

Fire – the four-step element program

The Fire element is all about honesty, bluntness, and a passion for truth. You say what everyone else is afraid to say. When the element of Fire is burning strong, you have the courage or tenacity to stand in the face of pretense and politeness and still speak to the unspeakable. Fire maintains its optimism and approaches everything with a headfirst, energetic abandon. It is the part in all of us that willingly moves towards change. Fire transmutes dated systems into ashes, creating the possibility for something new to emerge.

As a collective, this century is like living in a Fire cycle – we constantly hear about wars, suicide bombers, wildfires, fossil fuels causing climate change, massive extinctions of species, etc. We are at a very critical moment in the history of humankind – a time we could easily perceive as hopeless and irreparable. Fire is hopeful no matter what. It is the ultimate ally for radical change. Fire does not burn itself, nor does sharing its flame with another diminish its power. The element of Fire lives to share and include one and all in their party. Fire sources both life and death, and demands that everybody join in. It is the element of Fire that shows up in challenging times, persuading us to trust intuition and develop faith. When the heat gets turned up – only that which is sincere and true will survive.

THE STEPS

1. **EXPLORE: Go inside and identify the element's energies and patterns in your life.**

2. **ARTICULATE: Put words to your elemental patterns – speak with a trusted witness, laugh about it together.**

3. **INVESTIGATE: Acknowledge the strengths and shadow-sides. Identify and get familiar with your elemental lessons.**

4. **TRANSFORM: Begin a practice to create a new paradigm.**

Fire people are often labeled at a young age for either being really good or really bad, which contributes to their natural shyness. They are loud, boisterous and, therefore, often self-conscious. This is why they stand up for the underdog – because they always stood out. They are noticeable – we all stare into the fire. It's their simple presence that elicits jealousy. Anyone with strong Fire will tell you they find just as many people being attracted to them as those repelled by their heat. Only a few can keep up with people who have a lot of fire. If you have a generous amount of Fire and you can stand out without being self-conscious, this is your gift. This is what makes it easy for you to gain respect and fulfillment because you are outspoken and a leader.

> If you have a generous amount of Fire, having the courage to stand out without being self-conscious will make it easier to gain respect and fulfillment.

Nothing bums you out more than being ignored. Although you crave the attention and acknowledgment of others, you don't always admit to it. Why don't you admit it, Fire? You do love to be seen. The attention gets you in trouble. When your Fire element is honest about its need for attention and respect and your humor is available, you are easier to handle. There is nothing like you being transparent and letting us hear your disclosures of raw honesty.

Let's be honest: this Fire element elicits competition. You dress in colors and are bold. When the heat of Fire is showing off, all our shadows are triggered. We get jealous or competitive. Fire scorches those who get too close, because you lack the advanced communication skills to speak to your emotional content. You get angry first and then regret it later. When mature, Fire's temper and demeanor mellows and becomes more focused, creating a gift of intense and inspiring honesty. Fire people are healers and seers. We all love to be on the receiving end of Fire's energy when it is you doing your enthusiastic cheerleading. Being loved by a fire person makes everyone else's love dull in comparison.

Fire people are best suited for work where they can act as catalysts for change or sell you something. Fire keeps things stirred up – fast moving, it hates when it's all going too smoothly. They love drama – but again may not admit to this. Wherever they go, some great tale will follow. You're always ready to fly off to your next adventure. Goals that can be achieved quickly appeal to you. However, you're also inclined to lose interest just as quickly once the initial excitement fades or becomes routine. And when that happens, you're outta there. But in your haste you don't always remember what you've learned – especially, the boo-boos. Admit it, Fire: you too, can screw up.

Learn to finish what you start, or ask for help from those that can show you how. When Fire is willing to learn from the past, laugh at the ouches and embrace the "It would have been better if…" you are well on your way to earning a Ph.D. in the school of hard knocks.

Fire doesn't come with an off switch. Or at least it takes time to find it. Think of fire in nature: we try to douse the flames by pouring on water or covering with dirt. Fire doesn't know how to put itself out. It is wildly ambitious and thinks it is invincible. You may not know when to stop or even recognize when you are so far out in front that you are standing alone. If this is you, don't forget that your "throwing caution to the wind attitude" may feel reckless to those around you. At worst, you lose your energy with a sense of failure and you eat too much or party too hard and lose your steam.

Fire is very kinetic and physical – activity is the food that nourishes you. If this element is strong, you are well suited to the spontaneous side of life. Your energy must keep moving. Obviously, you are well suited for anything that keeps the heat up, whether it is a spin class, martial arts, motorcycles, or doing yoga every day. If not, the Fire element has the uncanny knack of becoming sluggish. If the Fire goes out, in comes depression, obesity, and addictions – when Fire is dysfunctional, it is very dysfunctional! Exercise is the quickest way to fire up your energy when depression or lethargy has come to roost.

> Fire is very kinetic and physical – activity is the food that nourishes your soul.

If you have abundant Fire, you trust your intuition. Always simmering, the Fire element can lead you to sudden bursts of inspiration and thrust you into action. You don't waste a lot of emotional feelings worrying over trifles or others' melodramas. Fire has a temper that erupts at the slightest irritation but then rapidly burns out. Your impulsive nature doesn't mean you should trample on other people's feelings or emotions, but that's what happens when you're so afraid of losing your freedom – or being, God forbid, bored. You ought to be the party planner, the aerobic teacher, or take some acting classes.

Too much Fire – you run the risk of being an overindulgent freedom lover who can't commit and is always looking for the fun, even at the expense of their own health. You forget to follow through and be responsible and get labeled the lazy fun machine.

Too little Fire – the humor is gone, independence is barely experienced and a sense of hopelessness follows you around.

Fire Energies and Key Words

- Needs to move energy in athletic ways
- Enthusiastic, passionate
- Impulsive, hot temper
- Inspirational
- Drama queens and kings
- Likes to have fun, energy, childish or childlike
- Doesn't like to be bored
- Sexual
- Colorful and bold
- Feisty – can't wait for a fight
- Stands up for the underdog
- Intuitive
- Enthusiasm
- Indulgent, "More, please!"
- Inspirational
- Ruthlessly honest
- Needs to be noticed
- Leader – doesn't want to sit still or follow
- Craves attention
- No off button; don't know when to stop
- Love of life
- Self-conscious
- Short-lived anger; fast and impulsive reaction
- Insecure at times, overly confident other times
- Honesty – blunt and philosophical, great one-liners
- Loves starting something new
- Ultra-independent – Rebel with a cause
- Endless optimist
- Philosophical
- Graduate of school of hard knocks

Strengths of Fire

- The ability to generously be a catalyst and inspiration for change
- Lots of life force
- Natural charisma that inspires others to listen or follow unquestionably
- Knack for attracting people and circumstances that are beneficial
- Fearless courage, and energy that does not stop
- A magnetic force field that attracts exactly what is needed in the nick of time
- The gift of intuition

Shadow of Fire

- Deception; can rationalize anything; tend to embellish or exaggerate
- Competitive without heart
- Egomania, self-centered, know-it-all
- Fiercely independent, self-reliant and self-indulgent
- Anger issues; violent outbursts, rage
- Hate details and often do not finish what you start
- Impatient with others who can't keep up
- Getting in trouble in the past can lead to fears of getting caught
- Self-importance and pride
- Unable to censor or be discriminatory with communication

Healthy Fire is cultivated when you learn how to regulate with ease the fierce but caring beast inside and can summon the awesome power of creative spontaneity through the psychological wisdom of an open heart. You are a great teacher and student of life.

Here are the big questions when you EXPLORE Fire:

- How do you serve your mission and gifts vs. the drama and boredom?
- Do you take time to look back, and learn from past mistakes? And not blame the other.
- How can you be sensitive to others and embrace the emotional side?

- Is it okay to tell your truth even if it means creating disharmony?
- How can you be in relationship and not lose your freedom?
- How can you be gentle and remain powerful?
- Can you stand up for yourself without being demanding and judgmental?

Take time to reflect and identify the habitual patterns and elemental energies of Fire that are part of your life story. Like the thought that, "I am too much." Or, "No one lets me be me." "I just want to have fun." Without judgment or becoming defensive, realize how much you do drama. Begin to identify the core beliefs and stories that you repeat. Fire needs honesty to change the old story. Put on some music, dance, shout, punch a pillow. It is a great practice for Fire to learn how to freely move their energy. Have a good laugh, and enjoy the awareness that you are just human like everyone else.

> Fire needs energy so metabolize what you are learning ... dance, shout, punch a pillow.

Review the elemental survey (fire) you completed earlier on: to what degree are you in touch with the element of Fire? Whether low or high, spend a few moments reflecting on where fire exists in your daily life. Get curious about the themes and situations where fire is alive or where you shut down.

Now use the Observer to see your patterns. Ask yourself, "How has my impulsiveness been naive?" "Do I use humor or defensiveness when the inner critic is awakened?" Often where you feel caught is where your Fire is being used by your ego to keep the old story running. Often when your Fire element is out of sync, it gathers evidence to justify your actions and discounts the feelings and emotions of others.

Take it one step further. Read the description of Fire people. Reflect again and talk about what else about your behaviors and patterns you are now aware of. Remember to turn off the ego, your internal critic and judge, and switch on the Observer, your compassionate soul, and witness your human self.

Now *ARTICULATE* and voice your Fire elemental patterns. Find a trusted companion and then take center stage and ask them to record your thoughts. Give yourself permission to be loud and boisterous. When you are finished ask them to read out loud what they have recorded. Just listen and let your Fire experience the warmth you generate. Fire hates to be mundane

FIRE people will relate to the following:

- I thrive expending physical energy
- I am outspoken and frequently say things that get me in trouble
- I am enthusiastic and passionate
- People would like to turn my volume down, or they think I'm too intense
- It is easy for me to laugh and find the humor in life
- I am deeply into philosophy and/or spirituality
- I inspire others to take action
- People get mad at me – anger can be an issue, either my own or that of others
- I can be the life of a party
- I fight for the underdog and/or love to argue and debate

and hates going slow. Be blunt and tell the truth about your patterns with a sense of humor. Laughing at yourself is the key to your freedom.

To *INVESTIGATE* your elemental lessons, turn off Fire's natural tenacity to think they already know the answer and take the attitude of an apprentice who is gathering data and learning a new skill. Ask questions, and explore your habits and patterns. Fire doesn't mind being knocked to their knees. They are the greatest students of life once they decide they are interested in the topic at hand.

Beware of your need for attention and acknowledgment and watch out for where your ego has captured you and turned your plight into drama central. Your challenge is to know your soul is joyful with or without others' attention. Seek insight and explore places where you have become depressed, lazy or lost interest. Practice saying, "I am just a normal human being and I can make mistakes." Give your soul permission to be proud of your fierce and sometimes misunderstood fire. Showing a little softness and emotions doesn't

> Beware of your need for attention and acknowledgment and watch out for where your ego has captured you and turned your plight into drama central.

put the fire out, it merely helps to start to temper the heat.

Get familiar with the strength of Fire and its shadow.

The key to sparking your Fire without starting a bonfire is to be more perceptive of the world around you. Fire people often have the reputation of being heartless or know-it-all's. You see, fire doesn't believe something just because everyone else does. However, that doesn't preclude you from slowing down long enough to listen. If you're always rushing to the next adventure, you are short-changing yourself and miss out on developing your skills to their full extent. If you aren't open to feedback, you miss out on life's little book of instructions and wisdom from others. Feedback gives you the very food to nourish your flame. Fire needs Air. Air is the artist of feedback. The arrogant Fire will lessen when you understand there are others who have something to offer. As Fire evolves, it gains self-awareness and the ability to laugh at itself.

Fire is the element that wants you to wholeheartedly enjoy the spontaneous ride you are on. It continues to nudge you along where angels fear to tread. Can you share your zest for life and fully experience the emotions and monotony that accompany life? You are here to trust your magic, and know you are a magnetic force field at best. At worst, your dreams are too big to be real and you are hurting people with your ego.

As you honestly identify the elemental lessons of Fire in your life, you will begin to develop empathy for human nature. Slowing down and taking the steps to own and then release your old patterns can be a challenge for Fire. You will think you are above all this. A first step is to give yourself permission to be human. I do have an ego. I am bossy. I do need attention. Giving your human self permission to be ruthlessly honest and vulnerable is your key to wisdom.

Permissions for Fire

- I can use my "off button" and know when to stop.
- I love change and can let my soul shine bright and enjoy it.
- I am open to commitment.
- I know that being big, independent, and successful doesn't make me too much to handle.
- I have the courage to be disruptive and not get in trouble.
- I can think and be out of the box and still be accepted.
- I am unique and labels don't define me.

- Feedback nourishes me and I am open to hearing from others.
- I will ask for what I need when I want attention.
- I am ok being outrageous and bold.
- I can let people know my intentions as well as be aware of how they are received by others.
- I will communicate with an open heart.
- I will keep going and not let fear stop me.

Now it is time to *TRANSFORM* and change the old story. You might:

- Ask for what you need – don't demand.
- Practice asking and giving feedback. Listen without defensiveness. Listening will help you.
- Expand your ability to believe your own opinion and see another's point of view.
- Enjoy the give and take of working with others.
- Not everything needs changing.
- Learn how to say, "Sorry, I was wrong."
- Know when to stop.

The right use of Fire is to stand in the face of catastrophe while keeping your heart open and maintaining faith, even when every thing seems disastrous. The open heart is a healthy Fire that says, "Regardless of rejection, I still love life, and nothing will turn my face away from love." The right use of Fire is also about knowing how to use anger as a proactive impulse to create change, rather than using anger to destroy.

If you wish to bring the element of Fire into balance or to create a practice to maintain stable healthy Fire, here are some suggestions to get you started.

Meditation

Meditation is a useful way to settle the energy of Fire. Taking time each day to "just be" allows your energy to be inspired and focused. Walking meditation is a great way to energize the practice and experience meditation in action. For most, walking meditation increases body awareness, which can add intense enjoyment for those with high energy. For anyone with Fire as an issue, Kundalini Yoga is a specific tool that really helps balance the Fire element.

Exercise

Exercise is the quickest way to fire up the body when there is depression or lethargy. Go slow and don't be discouraged; it may take some time, but once the regimen is in place, it is much easier to sustain health. You must exercise for your well being!

Experiment with New Styles of Communication

There are many ways to get your point across. Learn to have difficult conversations effectively. Take communication classes. You have a tendency to burn bridges and cut people out when you are done with them. Revisit old friends and open your heart to what you may have done to contribute to the story.

Learn to Fight Fair

Learning how to argue and fight in a way that's creative and gets you closer to the person you're fighting with will be an indicator of the right use of Fire. Saying you are sorry and stopping when others ask you to stop is an important skill for Fire. You are used to your intensity and may not fully recognize your impact. Being able to separate your intention from your impact is a great first step.

Experience Joy and Humor Every Day

Remember life is full of joy. Try singing or dancing. Seek out good news and happy tales. Find someone you can laugh with and who enjoys your sense of humor. All of these are ways to ignite Fire's natural optimistic life force. Find time to appreciate those who inspire you. Being immersed in joy is a great way to transfer from the school of hard knocks into the school of adventure and excitement.

> The key to sparking your Fire without starting a bonfire is to be more perceptive of the world around you.

Chapter 18

FIRE WOMEN

I am a vital and passionate person; I love to dress up, shine, and sparkle. I love attention and I don't often know how to hold back. There are times when I wish that I were more demure and soft, but when it comes right down to it, I just have to let it all go and speak my mind. If someone asks my opinion about their looks, their abilities, or their relationship – I tell the truth. I love honesty. I am a strong person, and assume that others are too. I can't change this impulse, I have tried. Please don't ask me a question if you don't want my honest, blunt opinion.

I love to stay in shape. I can be an exercise-aholic. If I stop working out, I lose energy. When I eat I can *really* eat, when I party I *really* party, when I am sexual, it is hot. I love speed and dare-devil kinds of things. However, that really passes in adulthood.

At worst, I am a drama queen caught in the need for attention – which I will get through any means possible. I can be demanding. At my best, I am loving and joyful, the life of the party and the one who opens hearts because I am so authentic, human, and fun.

Please don't take offense at my need for attention. As soon as I am full up, when I have been given to, I will give back to you tenfold. It's true, just give me what I demand, and I will do the same for you. But please, don't stop giving in the middle of our movie without warning me because when I feel personally rejected, or neglected, I can be harsh. Underneath the bravado of my fire is a tender heart that only wants to love.

Assertiveness training was never something that I needed. As a kid, I never understood why I was called bossy. It's just that I know how to get things done, and when I see someone struggling, I assume that they need help and I should show them how things are done.

Social

Even now, as an adult, I have two rhythms: either I shine brightly and am wild and uninhibited, or I am very shy and reserved until I have the stage or a safe place to show up in. When I am with my closest friends, I do not hold back – especially if they are Fire people themselves, people who aren't intimidated or afraid of my power. It is with my equals that I show my vulnerability, and it only happens rarely.

A little bit of encouragement goes a long way with me. I am far more sensitive than I appear. I can sense the slightest indication of rejection by my women friends or my lover, and I react instantly. As soon as they are inattentive, or fail to call regularly, I know that something is up and I am concerned.

I am good at fueling friendships and family relations. I will call and ask, "Are you mad at me?" I often assume I did something wrong because my bigger-than-life personality must have innocently insulted someone. Over-communicating is not easy for me, I like to bottom-line things, say things flat out and get on with the fun. This can offend people.

I will not let others take advantage of me, or my loved ones, and if they do, I respond quickly. For example, if someone criticizes me or someone I care about, it feels like I have been slapped in the face, and I impulsively retaliate. I can be hypersensitive to injustice and disloyalty and I always support the underdog. I stand up for what is important and encourage others to do the same; I cannot pretend, or casually walk away when something is not right. Through my behavior I am setting an example as a role model of integrity. Honor means everything to me.

Relationships

I long to be understood and loved. I want to be sent flowers, gifts, and love letters. These simple acts of kindness send me into ecstasy. If I am not recognized for my efforts, for my creativity, my love and support, I get pissy – which you'll know instantly because I am not reluctant to complain or even brashly swear in a passionate moment. I will let you know, in no uncertain terms, that you have hurt my feelings, are taking advantage of me, and need to reconsider your behavior.

Unless a man's personality is equal to mine, I can overpower him and we will not know what went wrong. I often play the caretaker for the entire family. Unless the father of my children is able to hold his own, as the mother I take on the primary role. When I feel that I have given too much and am spent, I can get very irritable and even caustic. I need lots of appreciation and applause to feed me. Someone saying, "Thanks, I love you," with a hug can dramatically change my attitude.

I was a tomboy when I was growing up. When I saw a boy whom I liked I thought it appropriate to tell him I liked him. I even asked guys out for dates. When I realized that the boys were competing with me, and that I was scaring them off, I either shied away or went deep inside myself.

I am eternally loyal and true-blue when it comes to love. I will flirt, but I know how to keep my heart on target and not cross lines. I am a monogamous woman and demand the same from my lover.

Family

I am a great mom for a kid, a pet, or even a plant. I am attentive and caring and will do anything for those I love. Above all other accomplishments, my kids are the pride and joy of my entire life, and I have known how important parenting is since I was a kid.

My loyalty to my parents is absolute. I am often the one to caretake them in their declining years. It is easy for me to take responsibility for helping any family member who *needs* me. I am (undyingly) loyal, and will go the extra mile for my family or friends. I put myself in the shoes of the helpless and know that I would want someone to help me. Often I have been accused of selfishness. I have never understood why people call me that. It seems to me that I am always concerned about the welfare of others. I talk about my kids all the time. For good or bad I talk about my spouse constantly. I am an open book.

In my early years, my favorite song was, "ME! ME! ME!" Aging serves me well. Once I have been acknowledged either publicly or privately, I no longer demand as much attention. All I want is for my children to be successful and for my name to be recognized. When that is fulfilled, I feel satisfied.

Work

I am an inspirational teacher, leader, and initiator. I am not afraid to try something new. I am always thinking up creative ways to sew, cook, dress, and help people. I have my own style of decorating, and when you visit my home you will no doubt notice my creativity. Please do, it hurts my feelings if you don't.

Anything I do, I pour my entire self into. I will work longer and harder then anyone else, and let everyone know that it was me at the helm. I like to toot my own horn just in case no one else will. My signature is big and obvious.

I am a good boss. You will get a big bonus from me whenever I sense that you are giving more than expected. I will be loyal to you if you follow my lead, but it might be hard for you when you think you are ready to take over; I am not good at sharing the limelight.

I have always found women's rights worth fighting for. I find it hard to understand why a woman should be paid less than a man. Often, men frustrate me – and I express it freely. Luckily, I have what it takes to command respect and so it doesn't alienate them.

I suspect that people talk behind my back. Please be careful with my feelings. It isn't good to have me on the wrong side of you or your project. The influence of my "big energy" is felt even if I am not around.

Chapter 19

FIRE MEN

Alive and kicking, that's me. I put the pedal to the metal, give my all to the moment and deal with the consequences later.

You will notice me. I know how to get what I want when I want it. I am blunt and straightforward, and I speak the truth without the societal censors that make for tact and diplomacy. Impulse grabs my heart, stirs my groin, and compels me towards my goal without restraint. Once I am on a roll, it's hard for me to find the off button.

I am full of surprises. I even shock myself sometimes.

But here's the interesting thing; **I am shy**. I seem self-assured because I speak out and assume the role of leader – but behind all that Fire is a sensitive kid who is just waiting for someone to judge me for my impulsive behavior and tell me to tone it down or chill out. People have been doing this to me since I was a kid, so even though I might seem immune to people's comments, the truth is, I live with a low-grade insecurity that people are bothered by me.

The good news is that I have the endurance and stick-to-it-ness to push through my fears. I excel at acting, athletics, spiritual/political leadership or sales. I am good at anything that requires courage and inspiration. I can turn up the volume, be loud and expressive, convincing you that voting for me is a must. You will undoubtedly buy from me, applaud me, or agree with me as I sweep you away into our moment together.

I am competitive. I can run farther, jump higher, and compete tirelessly when it comes to physical challenges. As a young person, it was difficult to get me tired out. Any Fire person knows that the more energy we spend, the more we get. If I don't move and or talk or initiate – I get bored. I lose energy through being relaxed – I gain energy from spending it. The more I exercise, the better I will feel.

The same is true with money. I love to spend. I am generous to a fault. I have learned how to share because I know that there is always enough for everyone. I feel angry and frustrated when others are not open to sharing and they hold back. Cheap people or depressed people are not my kind of folk.

Social

I'm really good at stirring the pot. If I can find someone to play with – with words, or to flirt with, or sing or party with – I'm happy.

I just want to have a good time and include all the friends I can. Feeling good is what I am all about. Happiness, drama, and enthusiasm are my essences. I have a contagious sense of joy. If someone doesn't want to join in, or they are party poopers, it is hard for me to not call them out, which is why sometimes the quieter, mild personality will find me overbearing.

My very favorite thing is to laugh and to make others laugh. The fun of life must be in focus or I get pissed off and want to do something wild and crazy to get things going. Practical jokes are my specialty. Candid Camera was designed by a Fire person. Let's do the strangest thing and publicly humiliate someone, all in the name of humor. I can't handle it when things are calm and orderly for too long.

I want to be in the middle of whatever is happening, I don't want to miss a thing. I love to be center stage, and can't handle the sidelines for too long. I will call attention to myself in some way or another. I will eat more candy, eat more cake, and party harder than most. I will burn the candle at both ends. Candle – fire, I get it. I am inappropriate at times, even goofy if I am too intoxicated. I do love to drink. It is hard for me to apply discipline and tone down even when someone has told me to do so.

It's great when I am happy, but when I am blue, it is equally intense. I suffer from extreme emotional states, but am unlikely to open up easily. When I get depressed, I'll only tell you if we are really close. Once or twice in my life I am likely to fall desperately in love and want to sing from the rooftops, but I have learned not to let such emotions have their way with me entirely. When I was young, I was a lot like Zorba the Greek. I wish that people knew that my outlandish behavior was an attempt to keep the fires burning and to wake people up to honesty and integrity. I am not trying to stir the pot to be disruptive. I am simply looking for those people with enough humor and joy to participate with me to make this planet a bit brighter. Please don't think that I am trying to hurt you when I tell you the truth as I see it. I am just being myself in my own fiery way. My true impulse comes from a passionate fire in my belly that will never go away.

Relationships

I am a person who needs relationship. When I was young it appeared that I set myself up for rejection. Rejection was familiar to me in my twenties. Until I have a real friend, mentor, or partner who supports me unconditionally, this pattern will repeat itself. But as soon as I have a strong alliance, I can find the calm.

I am an ardent lover. Passion and the sexual urge follow me throughout my life. At times I have been controlled by testosterone. Aging serves me well. When the physical impulse is less demanding, I am less compulsive. A raging fire is more attractive as it cools down. Like a good bottle of fire-water, I get better as I get older.

I am loyal when I am truly in love – anything less than the real stuff and I can wander. I have been hurt by disloyalty myself. This is a very sensitive topic that I cannot talk about. It is easier for me to get angry than to express my sadness.

Family

I am so impressed with my kids. I speak of them often, although it seems to them that I'm not paying enough attention – and when I am paying attention it's only to let them know how they can do things better. It's true that I tend to be bossy. It's just that I have very clear ideas about what they ought to be doing, and I gladly offer these ideas. I'm just trying to be helpful, though over the years I've come to realize that it's my ears and my time my kids want, not my opinions and my expectations.

It's hard for me to stay quiet when there are truths just under the surface. In my family I have to speak to what is really going on. If someone is having an affair and we all know it, I want to talk about it. I am not a socially appropriate personality – and don't want to be either.

My independence and crazy schedule has always prevented me from "being" around. "Doing" is what I am best at. Despite the fact that I am fast at everything I do, I am a slow learner when it comes to relationship and family. I am such a big personality, and use my single-eyed point of view to see the world. As I learn to slow down – with age – I begin to accept that mine is not the only opinion that matters and my attention to my family's feelings increase. Trust me, I will be humbled. It happens to all Fire men. Women are my greatest teachers.

Work

At work, I am a self-directed person. I am usually the boss, the lead actor, the best salesman; or I will quit. It's hard for me to be held back. I can appear very impatient. Teachers, bosses, even friends get mad at me, saying that I am arrogant and too strong for my own good. My personality softens as I reach some accomplishments. Through my successes, I learn to believe that I really am good at things. This is when I stop seeking approval and can quiet down quite a bit.

My success comes to me early on because I am very creative. I can quickly suss out the easiest, fastest route to any task at hand, and make it happen. I know how things should run. Change is easy for me. I can implement it, teach it, and problem-solve effortlessly.

My career can change radically in a ten-year span. I will try many projects and finally return to what I know best.

Conclusion

This is my life's message. I am a fire starter and I care deeply about who YOU are, and the Earth's well being. Take my words to heart.

Come away appreciating how much you as an individual matter. Your unique voice and essence are vital to the collective. We are a tapestry, and your thread and flavor are so important to our collective strength and to the sustainability of our species. We cannot pass through this historical moment without your full presence.

I don't write this lightly. As an astrologer I can tell you that we're swiftly moving into a major crisis. There are indicators to say that the world as we knew it is over. Just like in 1776 when the revolution began in America – there was a planetary alignment then that is repeating itself now, the first time since then. In 2011, Saturn was in Libra, and Uranus was in Capricorn – an inner revolution trying to emerge. This cycle will last for years.

The inner world is the last frontier; how we talk to ourselves, our internal dialogue, how much we celebrate this life and our expressions, how lovable we feel we are, and most of all, how worthy we each are. If you can fall in love with who you are and fully express yourself living inside your elemental nature – I promise, you are making a great contribution!

> If you can fall in love with who you are and fully express yourself living inside your elemental nature – I promise, you are making a great contribution!

It's an unusual time in history. We in North America have left behind our relationship with the basics – Water, Air, Earth, and Fire. When was the last time you sat in front of fire? When was the last time you drank fresh water from the mountains? When was the last time you walked to get your food? We rarely do ceremony and acknowledge the sacred in these simple ways.

We don't drink from the mountain stream any more – we pour our water into plastic containers from artificial sources that contain chemicals and supplements because we have polluted the source. We have an energy crisis because we no longer know how to use our natural power. We depend on energy drinks to get us moving. We use all kinds of artificial sources to keep us happy and healthy. From the Observer's point of view, it's not a bad thing, it's just a fact.

The air has been compromised because of the numbers of us driving. We have lost the feel of the earth under our feet. It is so much easier to jump into a car than to touch Mother Earth's back.

Simply put, we have lost our connection not only with the elements of the natural world but our ability to honor this life as a sacred experience. Secondly, there have never been so many people alive at one time in the history of our planet, and we do not have the resources for all of us over time, nor are we implementing new ways for the future to prepare for what is required to share and care. Period. Full stop. Fact. This is not debatable. We live with business as usual – but not forever.

We need to get fired up and change our ways. We pay other people to display and embody Fire for us. In fact, we pay more money to actors and athletes than any other profession. It is so much easier to have an Olympic master show us their Fire than for us to do it ourselves. We sit at the television and passively watch – this is a modern-day phenomenon alive everywhere.

We've lost our Air, as so many of us primarily communicate not with our tongues but with electronic devices – letting our thumbs do the talking. The things we've done to this Earth – fracking, GMOs – this is the first time in history that we've actually altered the seeds. What a powerful metaphor. We have altered everything natural including our hormonal balance, a man's sexual performance, and the tightness of our skin.

Like Hansel and Gretel who scatter breadcrumbs on the path, we are trying to find our way home. If we can even *find* our way back, I wonder what kind of home will we come back to? Our future seems dim to say the least. The young adults are talking about extinction and zombies – words we never used until this generation.

It is imperative that we get back to basics and get in touch with our own elemental, hands-on nature. Water is wet, Fire is hot, Earth is rock solid and Air is everywhere. This will never change. So how do we return to this wisdom of our elders and honor these vital elements from the ground level? It's simple. You can do it with your own unique expression of how you care for and how you talk to yourself.

Change starts at home. The key is to wake up the Observer in you – that's what this book, *The Missing Element, Compassion for the Human Condition* is all about – to notice where we are stuck, stand away from the judgment and take a different stand.

The four stories you read here are about a group of people who lived their lives with a desire to grow and change. They mastered the primary elements in their lives – thereby healing themselves, inspiring others, and making a difference.

Kenny, incarcerated, learned how to use the power of his mind – Air – to get him through twenty-seven years of prison. He knew that he didn't belong locked up for that long and he could have become shut down and angry. Instead he focused on the power of his mind and his faith to see him through. Charlie, the firefighter, angry and pained over the death of his friends, incorporated the wisdom of Water – emotion – to open himself up so that he could feel into his grief, forgive the people who killed his friends and move on.

Ann and Dave – true Earth people – learned how to share their resources with their staff and their community because they knew that the money they were making wasn't theirs to keep. Ann, who had come from a hard background, could have easily been broken or bitter. Instead she soothed her own wounds by becoming a true Earth mother; compassionate and generous.

Myra and Drew Goodman, and Colette, all took their Fire and made choices to go down the uncharted path. Colette went from being a woman who had been gang-raped and turned alcoholic, to becoming a famous psychic, channeling her Fire and burning it brightly and in service. Myra and Drew went against the odds and took their bold, fiery ideas for organic farming into a sustainable, successful business when everyone told them it couldn't be done. All of them woke up and took their lives into their own hands.

Like these people, each one of us has the power to create an energetic vibrancy through our personal expression, which will impact everything. These are individuals who made a huge difference. You can too. All you have to do is be yourself in full bloom.

We can't continue to live on this gorgeous rock like it's a hotel and the staff will clean up after us. We *are* the staff! We each need to understand what our part is, who we are as individuals; and where we are weak we need to come into more balance. The revolution is within. You can change our future by simply healing yourself.

It is my dream that we all wake up. But what does that mean? To realize that you matter, that you are not just one of many who can continue doing business as usual and sleepwalk right past your destiny. You are an exceptional individual. Believe me when I tell you: you are not a mistake, you are divinely orchestrated. It is true – and life is counting on you.

Nothing in this life matters more to me than to return to the wisdom of the elders and to absorb their teachings: honor the four directions, stand on the land with respect, and most of all, realize that Water, Air, Earth, and Fire are the gods embodied right here and now. We are the demi-gods in training. We must honor the elements. Our survival as a species and as individuals requires our attention.

Without the elements we are nothing, and without being in relationship to them, our human creation will crumble. It's simple: we cannot live without Water, Air, Earth, or Fire, and not one can be left out. I hope you can see how simple and true these words are and will take a look at your heart and soul and remember your role.

Aho Mitakuye Oyasin

> Honor the four directions,
>
> stand on the land with respect,
>
> and most of all, realize that
>
> Water, Air, Earth, and Fire
>
> are the gods embodied
>
> right here and now.

Appendix

THREE WAYS TO DEVELOP ELEMENTAL WISDOM

A powerful 90-minute process that I use in my work is an easy way to facilitate understanding of the Missing Element. This process is called 4E and it allows you to understand through a direct experience of elemental wisdom, (a) the Element that is in your way, (b) which Element is stronger, and, (c) how to bring yourself back into balance. In the 4E process, based on Parts therapy, you sit in each Element and give yourself the voice of that part of you and find out its needs, strengths, and weaknesses.

4E is the descendant of a process and product called **The Symbols Way** (TSW). It was developed as a means for men and women to directly feel their life calling in their current age and stage of life. TSW assists you to discern the way forward in times of transition as well as over thresholds and through choice points. Many describe the process as an initiation into a new phase of their journey, something that is deeply rooted in their essential nature.

To connect to a trained coach who can guide you through this process, contact Barbara Cecil:

endingsandbeginnings.com

4E is my differentiation of this process and is focused on dissolution of psychological barriers that keep one stuck in repeating patterns and unable to move forward. My background as a therapist and astrologer inform the process as a way of helping to fill in Missing Elements that inhibit growth. Contact Debra Silverman at:

debrasilvermanastrology.com

The third relative in this family is the **Collective Symbols Way Process**. This was developed as a resource for teams, organizations, and groups that are in specific infection points in their evolution. Professional guides who are trained in organizational learning offer this framework as a way to perceive emerging potential and move into a future with confidence and sensitivity to a larger ecology of factors. Contact Dorian Baroni at:

dorianbaroni.com.

FINDHORN PRESS

Life-Changing Books

Consult our catalogue online
(with secure order facility) on
www.findhornpress.com

For information on the Findhorn Foundation:
www.findhorn.org